ALDOUS HUXLEY

ALDOUS HUXLEY

By

Alexander Henderson

New York

RUSSELL & RUSSELL

1964

FIRST PUBLISHED IN 1936
REISSUED, 1964, BY RUSSELL & RUSSELL, INC.
BY ARRANGEMENT WITH CHATTO & WINDUS, LONDON
L. C. CATALOG CARD NO: 64-20668
PRINTED IN THE UNITED STATES OF AMERICA

17882

To MARGARET

Mein und Dein

It is an unusual, and it may be unhappy, temperament that can always adjust itself to the ironic view. For that view necessitates on one side a certain mystical faith ; on another, a readiness to laugh at oneself, the acutest if not the wholesomest of pleasures ; on yet another, an extreme tolerance ; on another still, an immense pessimism.

George Saintsbury.

CONTENTS

Chapter 1

INTRODUCTION

Because we all know how to read, we imagine that we know what we read.   Enormous fallacy !—*Vulgarity in Literature.*

ALDOUS HUXLEY has been writing for nineteen years. During that time he has produced twenty-five works of the most varied kinds, in each of which is immediately perceptible a mind and a sensibility of a distinction uncommon at the present time.   There is no living author better worth re-reading.   No one who can better inspire one with the courage of Europe in the face of the American big-shots, Hemingway, Dos Passos, and Faulkner.   Few writers have more important things to say than Huxley, and none has a finer style, a politer malice, a deeper culture or a more secure artistry.

Huxley's serious reputation has, I believe, suffered from the fashionable and slightly scandalous success which attended certain of his novels.   Among the smart, up-to-date sections of London Society and intelligentsia *Antic Hay* was, when it appeared in 1923, the one book it was unforgivable not to have read.   At the same time the bigger public was shocked. It was reported by a popular London newspaper that *Antic Hay* had been burned by the Public Librarian in Alexandria because it ' smelled too strongly of the goat.'   The ' burning ' was, as I happen to know, a

piece of journalistic licence. But that imaginary bon-
fire in Alexandria has cast its indignant glow upon a
score of volumes.

Five, ten, fifteen years afterwards, Borough Coun-
cillors light upon one of Huxley's novels, and suddenly
fearful that their children may grow up better men
than they are, proclaim that though themselves above
corruption, nevertheless they consider that such books
should not be written. They may have a bad moral
effect on the young (*i.e.* prevent them from being like
father). And accordingly the book is banned from the
public library. There is nothing like a Borough
Councillor for stopping fun.

That, in 1935, is still the public reaction to Huxley.
It should be sufficient indication that he is one of the
most serious of living writers.

For the reviewers too there is a stock attitude.
With magnificent, if perverted tenacity they go on
year after year observing the Huxley of their own
creation, and complaining that they do not like it.
Their Huxley, then, is a pale-grey cardboard figure
labelled : ' Intellectual — slightly unpleasant.' The
first half of the tag appears to be inspired by the vanity
of the critic, the second by his tender solicitude for the
public. Time after time the reviewers complain that
Huxley is too intellectual, too puritan, too abstract, or
alternatively (in sudden panicky reaction), too voluptuous, concrete and obscene. And among reviewers of every class Huxley inspires plaintive
wailings that he is too intelligent, and anyhow, unlike
other writers.

It must be conceded that the reviewers are unfortunate in that they have not the time to re-read the whole of a writer's production on each occasion of noticing a new work. But ideally they should do so. It is not possible to criticize understandingly any given book unless one is familiar with its predecessors. To assess the growth of a mind it is necessary to know the beginning as well as the latest stage ; to know it fully, from every side, to see it retrospectively, as well as to have seen it prospectively.

Such a re-reading, such a thorough knowledge of the past would be particularly valuable in the case of Huxley, and it would dispose of the notions that because a man is intelligent, he is inhuman, because he is sceptical, he has no doctrine, and because he writes with style, he is therefore immoral.[1]

English literature is weak in what is possibly the only sort of criticism that matters : workshop criticism, technical examinations of the different jobs a writer has to do. Too often our criticism runs off into philosophical speculations, ethical divagations, or into patches of decorative but useless prose. Especially is this true of criticism of the art of fiction which until recently has hardly been subjected to conscious study.

[1] 'I myself have frequently been accused, by reviewers in public and by unprofessional readers in private correspondence, both of vulgarity and wickedness—on the grounds, so far as I have ever been able to discover, that I reported my investigations into certain phenomena in plain English and in a novel.'— *Vulgarity in Literature.*

I have always disliked that kind of criticism which treats of Hamlet as though he had a subconscious to be analysed, or a soul to be saved. This is the criticism which on a more popular level describes the characters of fiction as ' lovable ' or ' unpleasant '—as though it were the proper business of a character to be ' lovable,' or indeed anything at all but a number of words on paper. Hamlet is only so many lines of verse and prose. Who does not feel the pointlessness of Coleridge's criticism when he starts discussing why Hamlet acted as he did, and why he came to grief? He did so because Shakespeare intended the play to work out like that.

This kind of criticism which talks of fictions as though they were realities is little better than amateur criticism. It is that of the lending-library subscriber. She—it is usually a woman—will say of a novel or play : ' Don't you think X was horrid? But Y was marvellous, wasn't she? I like Y, but I don't think I could have done what she did, do you?' This might be taken as a tribute to the vividness of the author's creation, were it not that it is usually said of the works of Mrs. Barclay, rather than of those of Mrs. Woolf.

At the opposite extreme is the criticism which values a work merely in so far as it is a peep-hole on to the author's character, personal opinions, or experiences in love. This sort of criticism is to be found in books entitled *Sebastian Jones : The Man*, despite the fact that the only interesting thing about Jones is not his maleness, but his poetry. Doubtless works

of art can act as peep-holes on personality, but it is of
no profit to us to know the state of an individual's
psyche. What is interesting is the *procedure* of a
writer's art, its native peculiarities, excellences, weaknesses—the characteristics by which it may be recognized. Beyond that, in the case of a philosophic
essayist, the truth of his ideas, their value for action,
for life. The maleness of poets does not differ appreci-
ably from that of other men. Their love affairs are
much like those of grocers. Only strictly in their
capacity as poets are they worth elaborate study. And
that is a task seldom undertaken.

Huxley's own natural reticence and the impersonal
manner of his work have held off the *Sebastian Jones*
type of criticism. In dealing with Huxley's works
the usual formula has been to apply the ' unpleasant '
or ' lovable ' classification, and on the whole his
characters have been found unpleasant. From this
conclusion, it is but a step to such peculiar mis-
readings as :

> ' Is it surprising in the circumstances that Mr.
> Huxley is left with a puritanical disgust of life and
> a bleak cerebral pessimism ? ' (R. D. Charques:
> *Literature and Social Revolution*); or, 'His findings
> are always the same. Go where you like, " do
> what you will," you will never escape from the
> smell of ordure and decay' (John Strachey: *The
> Coming Struggle for Power*).

The only possible explanation for such remarks
must be that the authors simply have not read Huxley

with the care they would give, for instance, to D. H. Lawrence. Probably no important contemporary writer has been read with such superficiality, even by his most intelligent readers, as Huxley.

This is no doubt partly his own fault. His style invites to a swift, delicious glide. His irony charms continually. The firm easy movement of his prose lulls the mind into a quiet glow of admiration. With the reader thus drugged, Huxley can say anything and get away with it. Indeed it is his misfortune that he gets away with it too easily. Like Shaw he suffers from the consequences of providing too much jam with his pills. His readers will swallow pills indefinitely for the sake of the red, delicious jam, and there is so much of it, that they never notice the hard white pill in the centre, which indeed, drowned in raspberry, leaves them unpurged and asking for more.

Because he is so easy to read, Huxley has never been read carefully enough, and because of that his books have never been subjected to a thorough, serious criticism.

This essay is an attempt at a careful reading.

Chapter 2

BIOGRAPHICAL

Given a reasonable amount of luck, it is possible to live a
not intolerable life.—*Music at Night.*

I

Biography

To write an adequate biography of Aldous Huxley
it would be necessary, one feels, to write also of his
grandfather, T. H. Huxley, defender of Darwinism,
his father, Leonard Huxley, LL.D., and his mother,
Julia Arnold, with, consequently, some account of
Matthew and Thomas Arnold.   In short, to write the
history of two English families, alike, both of them,
in their substantial conformity to social convention
combined with their vivid nonconformity of the
intellect.

T. H. Huxley would have noted his grandson's
interest in science with warm approval, would possibly have felt a slight jealousy at the spectacle of a
command of irony and sarcasm even greater than his
own, and would have wished, perhaps, that his grandson might take a more personal part in the contro-
versies of the day.

Matthew Arnold, at least in his *Culture and Anarchy*
moods, could not have failed to read much of Aldous
Huxley's writing with the greatest pleasure, while

7

Dr. Arnold, though strongly disapproving of such irreverent and un-Anglican writings as the opening of *Antic Hay*, might have been compelled to admit and even admire the seriousness of his descendant's work.

One should even, I suppose, go back to T. H. Huxley's mother. For in her we can see one of Aldous Huxley's outstanding characteristics.

'Her most distinguishing characteristic,' says T. H. Huxley of his mother, 'was rapidity of thought. . . . The peculiarity has been passed on to me in full strength.'

It has been passed on no less to Thomas Huxley's grandson.

Besides rapidity of thought, a certain intellectual and spiritual toughness appears to characterize Aldous Huxley. A similar strength is no less observable in the grandfather, who, despite indifferent health for much of his life, lived to be seventy and combined the raising of a numerous family with a vast amount of intellectual and moral work of the most exhausting kind. The story of T. H. Huxley's life, right from the beginning, with his future wife's years of waiting for him at the other end of the earth in Australia, has indeed the touching quality of some primitive, peasant epic of love, work, fighting and enduring faithfulness.

To indicate the environment of Aldous Huxley's youth, it will probably be sufficient to give a brief outline of his father's career.

Leonard Huxley was born in 1860, when his father, T. H. Huxley was thirty-five.   At the age of ten Leonard was sent to University College School in Gower Street.   Founded in 1830 by Lord Brougham, James Mill and Henry Hallam as a preparatory institution for the free-thinking University College which had been set up in 1827, the school, by reason of a similar doctrinal liberty, would obviously appeal to a sceptic like T. H. Huxley as suitable for his son. Leonard Huxley remained at U.C.S. till he was seventeen.

His subsequent education took place at Balliol College, Oxford, and St. Andrews University, of which he was later made an Honorary LL.D.   At the age of twenty-three he became assistant to Professor Lewis Campbell, professor of Greek at St. Andrews, and was afterwards assistant at Charterhouse.   He is best known, however, for his work on *The Cornhill Magazine*, which he edited for many years.   He was also literary adviser to Smith, Elder and Co., who founded the magazine.   Leonard Huxley died in 1933.

His chief works are the official *Life and Letters of T. H. Huxley*, a shorter, more popular biography of his father, the *Life and Letters of Sir Joseph Dalton Hooper*, and *The Letters of Jane Welsh Carlyle to her Family*.

Aldous Huxley was born on July 26, 1894, when his father was thirty-four.   He was the third son.

It has become the custom among biographers when

they reach the birth of their subject, to fill a page or two with a brisk summary of the world events contemporaneous with the birth, as though these diverse happenings in some way affected the infant mind.

It would surely be more valuable to inform the reader as to what was happening when the infant had begun to reach years of discretion and take an intelligent interest in the world about him. Heaven may lie about us in our infancy, but it is, surely, rather our father's and mother's idea of heaven than our own. This imposed heaven is, admittedly, of the greatest influence on one's character. And in writing this biography of Huxley I shall not omit certain significant details of the heaven of Huxley *père*.

But no less important is the heaven which Huxley *fils* first formed for himself. And to know that we want some idea of what the world was like in the years when he was first making serious contact with it, we must know what were the materials out of which Huxley constructed his own heaven.

The age at which one begins to explore the world of adults varies from individual to individual. If we take fourteen or fifteen as usual we shall not be far wrong.

Huxley was fourteen in 1908. What were the sort of events in the world which he would be likely to notice, or hear talked about? What were the social, literary and aesthetic influences to which he would be subjected?

In 1908 England not only was rich, but also felt rich. In the past twenty years the number of people with money in the bank had vastly increased. Since 1886 the number of cheques passing through the London Bankers' Clearing House had more than doubled. The country had become wealthy largely on foreign and imperial trade and investment, and it was the question of how best to continue these profitable activities which provided the finest subject of controversy of the age. The problem of Protection or Free Trade was settled in a thousand headlines. It was settled yet once again in 1906 when Sir Henry Campbell-Bannerman, the Liberal leader and Free Trader, became Prime Minister.

Along with the Liberals no less than twenty-nine Labour representatives managed to get into Parliament. For the best people this was a scandal. But it was a scandal which had been growing for some time. When in the last century Sir William Harcourt had said, in the House of Commons, ' we are all Socialists now,' it was felt to be a witticism in rather poor taste. Only Sir William's reputation as a sound lawyer and a Whig of the Old School made the joke at all permissible. After all, the M.P.s reflected, he could not really mean it. And of course, Sir William did not really mean it. What he meant was that the Socialists were coming on in the world. Which indeed they were, what with Hyndman, the Webbs, William Morris and G. B. Shaw, and Charles Booth's serial analysis of the London poor which from 1889 to 1902 provided the Socialists with volume after volume of unpleasant facts wherewith to challenge the capitalists.

These and other investigations showed that the life of the London poor was in fact ' nasty, brutish and short.' The conscience of the comfortable and educated was touched. Men of the sort of standing of Huxley's father worked in the slums and established University ' Settlements ' and Public School Missions.

With the development of social conscience went a decline in religious belief. Darwin and T. H. Huxley and the criticism of the Bible were proving to be more popular than the Book itself. It was a period when the high-minded were perpetually wrestling with their consciences, when the practice of abandoning prayer and the Deity, inaugurated in an earlier generation by such men as Moncure Conway, was spreading to the less distinguished.

At fourteen or fifteen when one begins to read adult literature, the really exciting writers are those nearest to one's own age—which means those of twenty-five to thirty. Further, one tends to read with most interest the books which these writers are themselves reading. In 1908 the tradition of the nineties, of what was called, with mysterious obviousness, ' the end of the century ' was still active, though in a somewhat changed form.

In the pre-war decade of this century the important things in English literary life were mostly French. During the nineties epoch about the only English writers a young man of taste could allow himself to read without losing prestige were Max Beerbohm, Dowson, Lionel Johnson and perhaps Thomas Gordon Hake, the little-known author of *Maiden Ecstasy* and *On the Powers of the Alphabet*.

But to read English writers at all was already an undoubted lapse from grace. For the really real thing you had to go to France. Baudelaire, Rimbaud, Verlaine, Laforgue and Anatole France had between them said what was, indubitably, the last word.

This feeling persisted on beyond the turn of the century, and Aldous Huxley assiduously read Anatole France and the French poets. The irony, the intellectual contempt of these writers for the gross practical world he found essentially congenial.

Huxley was particularly fortunate in that he had a strong interest in science to counteract the influence of the more futile developments of the nineties. The once really smart emotional state, that of feeling 'a little weary,' can have had slight appeal to him. But the interest in the fantastic, the rich and strange characteristic of the 'end of the century,' can be seen too in some of Huxley's short stories, such as *Cynthia*, *Eupompus Gave Splendour to Art by Numbers*, *The Death of Lully*, *The Young Archimedes*.

In writing about Aldous Huxley there is not much for the biographer to make play with. His life has not been picturesque in the obvious ways. The excitements are internal, the history psychological. It is a question of describing a mental development.

Fortunately he has himself in his different works

described, either directly or indirectly, the principal influences of his youth.

He was, as is generally known, educated at Eton and Balliol, and he appears to have enjoyed the education he received at those institutions.

'. . . as it happens,' he remarks, ' I have the kind of mind to which an academic training is thoroughly acceptable. Congenitally an intellectual, with a taste for ideas and an aversion from practical activities, I was always quite at home among the academic shades. Liberal education was designed for minds like mine.'

Elsewhere, however, on the teaching of mathematics at Eton, he comments unfavourably : '. . . yet I must insist, in my own defence, that the system of mathematical instruction of which, at Eton, I was the unfortunate victim, was calculated not merely to turn my desire to learn into stubborn passive resistance, but also to stifle whatever rudimentary aptitude in this direction I might have possessed.'

Oxford he liked because it left him at liberty to work in his own way, which is, as the students of other universities have found with some chagrin, a liberty that badly needs extending.

Oxford and Cambridge, he says, have ' by far the best system of teaching. It is possible at Oxford or Cambridge to obtain a degree without ever attending any lectures at all. (I myself never attended more than, at the outside, two lectures a week.) '

While at Oxford he was writing a good deal of poetry. His first volume, *The Burning Wheel*, was published by Blackwell in 1916 when he was twenty-two. *The Defeat of Youth* followed in 1918.

These early poems reveal a character intensely romantic and idealistic. They show Huxley to have been preoccupied with that inner conflict which he has dramatized in the characters of Denis in *Crome Yellow*, Walter Bidlake in *Point Counter Point*, and Bernard Marx in *Brave New World*.

A clear expression of this conflict between romantic idealism and physical desire is contained in the following poem from *The Defeat of Youth* :

THE ALIEN

A petal drifted loose
From a great magnolia bloom,
Your face hung in the gloom,
Floating, white and close.

We seemed alone : but another
Bent o'er you with lips of flame,
Unknown, without a name,
Hated, and yet my brother.

Your one short moan of pain
Was an exorcising spell :
The devil flew back to hell ;
We were alone again.

The same conflict is dealt with at greater length in the one-act play *Happy Families*, somewhat symbolist in manner, which is contained in the 1920 *Limbo*.

His intense life in the world of ideas and aesthetic beauty, and his slightly unhappy sense of ineffectiveness in the world of more grossly human contacts are both well shown in two poems from *The Defeat of Youth*. One is called *The Life Theoretic* :

> While I have been fumbling over books
> And thinking about God and the Devil and all,
> Other young men have been battling with the days
> And others have been kissing the beautiful women.
> They have brazen faces like battering rams.
> But I who think about books and such—
> I crumble to impotent dust before the struggling,
> And the women palsy me with fear.
> But when it comes to fumbling over books
> And thinking about God and the Devil and all,
> Why, there I am.
> But perhaps the battering rams are in the right of it,
> Perhaps, perhaps . . . God knows.

The other reads :

> Books and a coloured skein of thoughts were mine ;
> And the magic words lay ripening in my soul
> Till their much whispered music turned a wine
> Whose subtlest power was all in my control.
>
> These things were mine, and they were real for me
> As lips and darling eyes and a warm breast :
> For I could love a phrase, a melody,
> Like a fair woman, worshipped and possessed.
>
> I scorned all fire that outward of the eyes
> Could kindle passion ; scorned, yet was afraid ;
> Feared, and yet envied those more deeply wise
> Who saw the bright earth beckon and obeyed.
>
> But a time came when, turning full of hate
> And weariness from my remembered themes,
> I wished my poet's pipe could modulate
> Beauty more palpable than words and dreams.

All loveliness with which an act informs
The dim uncertain chaos of desire
Is mine to-day; it touches me, it warms
Body and spirit with its outward fire.

I am mine no more : I have become a part
Of that great earth that draws a breath and stirs
To meet the spring.   But I could wish my heart
Were still a winter of frosty gossamers.

In a broad generalization in *On the Margin*, Huxley
describes what was no doubt his own spiritual upbringing :

' With the disintegration of the solid ortho-
doxies,' he writes, ' Wordsworth became for many
intelligent, liberal-minded families the Bible of that
sort of pantheism, that dim faith in the existence
of a spiritual world, which filled, somewhat inade-
quately, the place of the older dogmas.   Brought
up as children in the Wordsworthian tradition,
we were taught to believe that a Sunday walk
among the hills was somehow equivalent to church-
going. . . .'

This Wordsworthian idealism — treated dramatically in *Those Barren Leaves*—made a deep impression on Huxley.   It was a childhood influence from
which it cost him some effort to escape, and the
marks of it are, I think, still perceptible in his work.
The influence shows itself in a tendency to over-
emphasize the rational, the materialist, in what is, in
fact, a mild over-compensation.

Together with Wordsworth went Ruskin.

'My parents . . .' says Huxley, 'had no great
love for the Oxford movement, but I was brought
up in the strait and narrow way of Ruskinism;
and so strict was my conditioning that it was not
till I was at least twenty and had come under the
influence of the aestheticians of a newer school that
I could perceive the smallest beauty in St. Paul's
Cathedral. Till then, its dome and round arches
acted on me like a Pavlovian bell: at the sight of
them I had shuddered, and the thought "How
ugly!" had immediately presented itself to my
consciousness.'

Intellectual caution was, Huxley says, a characteristic of his youth. He gives an interesting glimpse
of himself at the age of twenty-one, when he first met
D. H. Lawrence. The account is in his introduction
to Lawrence's *Letters*.

'I remember very clearly,' he says, 'my first
meeting with him. The place was London, the
time 1915 . . . he was on the point, so he imagined, of setting off to Florida—to Florida, where
he was going to plant that colony of escape, of
which up to the last he never ceased to dream. . . .
Before tea was over he asked me if I would join
the party, and although I was an intellectually
cautious young man, not at all inclined to enthusi-
asms, though Lawrence had startled and embar-
rassed me with sincerities of a kind to which my

up-bringing had not accustomed me, I answered yes.'

Huxley did not see a great deal more of Lawrence till 1926. But from that time till Lawrence's death they were often together. Huxley admired Lawrence very much. He seemed to him essentially different in kind from most other writers of his acquaintance. In another passage of the introduction to the *Letters* Huxley says :

' In a spasmodically kept diary I find this entry under the date of December 27, 1927 : "Lunched and spent the p.m. with the Lawrences. D. H. L. in admirable form. He is one of the few people I feel real respect and admiration for. Of most other eminent people I have met I feel that at any rate I belong to the same species as they do. But this man has something different and superior in kind, not degree." '

Lawrence's reaction to Huxley was one of affection for the man, but dislike for his books, which, nevertheless, he admired, though, as far as one can see, without greatly understanding just what Huxley was getting at.

Lawrence writes of *Proper Studies* in a letter to Aldous Huxley :

' I have read 70 pages with a little astonishment that you are so serious and professorial. You are not your grandfather's *Enkel* for nothing—that funny dry-mindedness and underneath social

morality.   But you'll say I'm an introvert, and no
fit judge.   Though I think to make *people* intro-
verts and extraverts is bunk—the words apply,
obviously to the *direction* of the consciousness or
the attention, and not to anything in the individual
essence.   You are an extravert by inheritance far
more than *in esse*.   You'd have made a much
better introvert, had you been allowed.'

In 1929 Lawrence writes to Lady Ottoline Morrell
from Bandol :

' Aldous and Maria were here for ten days or so
—neither of them very well, run down.   Aldous
with liver, and Maria going very thin and not
eating enough.   I think the *Counter Point* book
sort of got between them. . . . No, I don't like
his books : even if I admire a sort of desperate
courage of repulsion and repudiation in them.   But
again, I feel only half a man writes the books—a
sort of precocious adolescent.   There is surely
much more of a man in the real Aldous.'

Probably the most deeply important event in
Huxley's life was his three years of partial blindness
as a boy.   Cut off from ordinary activities, he
developed a detached, aloof attitude to life.   His
principal occupation was extensive reflection and
meditation on the information brought to him by
conversation, by books and by his physical sensations.

' I belong to the class of unhappy people,' he
says, ' who are not easily infected by crowd excite-

ment. Too often I find myself sadly and coldly
unmoved in the midst of multitudinous emotion.
Few sensations are more disagreeable. The defect
is in part temperamental, and in part is due to that
intellectual snobbishness, that fastidious rejection
of what is easy and obvious, which is one of the
melancholy consequences of the acquisition of culture. How often one regrets this asceticism of the
mind ! How wistfully sometimes one longs to be
able to rid oneself of the habit of rejection and
selection, and to enjoy all the dear, obviously
luscious, idiotic emotions without an after-
thought ! '

In noting the intellectual character of Huxley's
work, the physical, sensuous side should not be
neglected. Huxley is very like Rémy de Gourmont
in this respect. His acute intelligence is fed by a
vigorous sensuous awareness of the physical world.
Huxley would actually, I think, like to go further in
this direction. He would like to live even more
intensely the life of the senses, although from his last
book, *Beyond the Mexique Bay*, it looks as though he
had given up hope of being able to do so.

' The advance from primitivism to civilization,'
he says, ' from mere blood to mind and spirit, is a
progress whose price is fixed; there are no dis-
counts even for the most talented purchasers. I
thought once that the payment could be evaded, or
at least very greatly reduced; that it was possible
to make very nearly the best of both worlds. But,

this, I believe, was a delusion. The price that has to be paid for intellect and spirit is never reduced to any significant extent.'

In 1919 Huxley married Maria Nys, a Belgian. In the same year he was working on the editorial staff of *The Athenæum*. To that now extinct periodical he contributed a series of short essays—' middles '—which, it seems to me, must have had a decisive influence on the formation of his style. A number of these essays, which appeared anonymously, were afterwards published in *On the Margin*.

From 1920 to 1921 he was dramatic critic of *The Westminster Gazette*, a job which he did not greatly relish. He says of it :

> ' Once, in the course of an ill-spent life, it was my fate to go to the theatre some two hundred and fifty times in one year. On business, I need not add ; one would hardly do that sort of thing for pleasure. I was paid to go.
>
> By the end of the year—and, for that matter, long before our planet had completed its orbit round the sun—I had come to the conclusion that I was not paid enough ; that, indeed, I could never be paid enough for this particular job. I gave it up ; and nothing would now induce me to resume it.'

The short stories *Limbo* and the poems *Leda* appeared in 1920, and his first novel, *Crome Yellow*, in 1921. From that date his biography is largely a record of books published.

He has travelled widely, if not intensively, in India and Burma, Malaya, Japan and the U.S.A., and in Mexico, Guatemala, Honduras and the West Indies. ' With me,' he lightly confesses, ' travelling is frankly a vice.'

In Europe he has travelled much in Italy—a country whose plastic arts and landscape have been most important for his personal development.

Writing on the subject of ' Centenaries ' in the early 1920's he says : ' How much better they order these things in Italy ! In that country—which one must ever admire more the more one sees of it—they duly celebrate their great men,' etc., and proceeds to eulogize some of the more noisy popular manifestations of Fascism. The mood contrasts strongly with Huxley's present dislike of Fascism. The explanation, is, I think, that ten years ago he was able to ignore political questions, but now finds he cannot do so ; that they are too urgent. Apart from that, there is so much of interest in Italy, the works of nature and man are so often wholly admirable there, that even now it is possible to overlook the disabilities of the Fascist regime. Usually the Fascists leave one alone, and one has to be a very ardent democrat to feel spiritually oppressed in Fascist Italy. Italians still seem very charming people, though many who knew pre-Fascist Italy notice a change for the worse. Apparently a certain conflict is being set up in the Italian nature, a conflict between their natural impulse towards gaiety and inefficiency and their inculcated duty to attain a more than Roman ' gravitas.' It is rather like the effect of the Puritan movement in England.

Huxley's enthusiastic account of the *manifestazioni sportive* of a Fascist centenary celebration of Dante is too, I feel, by way of an attack on his own over-intellectual youth. The conflict between intellectualism and emotionalism runs through his whole life. It may be observed as well in the early poems as in *Brave New World*.

This inward dispute reveals itself in Huxley's attitude towards the question of personal freedom. In *Point Counter Point*, Philip Quarles, the intellectual, endeavours to settle down with his wife and child in the country. The child dies. Rustication loses its purpose, and Philip resumes the life of a wanderer, a detached spectator again. In some way it seems he is destined to this sort of life. That Huxley, similarly, has himself sometimes wanted to settle down, and become something other than what he is, is shown in a passage of *Jesting Pilate*, his diary of a journey to the East :

' I have always felt a passion for freedom. It is a passion which the profession of writing has enabled me to gratify. . . .

Professionally free, I have taken care not to encumber myself with the shackles that tie a man down to one particular plot of ground ; I own nothing, nothing beyond a few books and the motor-car which enables me to move from one encampment to another.

It is pleasant to be free, when one has enough
to do and think about to prevent one's ever being
bored, when one's work is agreeable and seems
(pleasing illusion !) worth while, when one has a
clear conscience of what one desires to achieve and
enough strength of mind to keep one, more or less
undeviatingly, on the path that leads to this goal.
It is pleasant to be free. But occasionally, I must
confess, I regret the chains with which I have not
loaded myself. In these moods I desire a house full
of stuff, a plot of land with things growing on it ;
I feel that I should like to know one small place and
its people intimately, that I should like to have
known them for years, all my life.'

But despite these desires, he has remained the
interested spectator, too anxious to see all the game
to risk playing in it for more than a moment or two.
He is essentially a solitary, and is aware that he is.
His religious life is one of solitariness. His recrea-
tions, reading and landscape painting, are solitary ones.
He has a great curiosity about human beings, but
dislikes social gatherings. He finds ' being up to date
and in the swim intolerably wearisome.' ' So,' he
says, ' I simply avoid most of the manifestations of
that so-called " life " which my contemporaries seem
to be so unaccountably anxious to " see." '
Writing of Lawrence, he is describing himself
when he says :

' He knew by actual experience that " the
writer " is an essentially separate being, who

must not desire to meet and mingle, and who
betrays himself when he hankers too yearningly
after common human fulfilments.'

Huxley was twenty when the war broke out in
August 1914. At that time only the very politically minded concerned themselves with the affairs
of foreign states. And Huxley was less politically
minded than most. The result was that he escaped
mentally from the war, without much difficulty, into
the world of books, of ideas and aesthetic beauty.
His first two books of poetry were published, in
fact, during the war years.

When it was over, however, he seems to have
experienced a mood of bitterness lasting for two or
three years. Two stories of the 1920 *Limbo—The
Farcical History of Richard Greenow*, and *Happily
Ever After*—combine mockery varying from the light
to the ferociously farcical with sharply felt tragedy.
Despair, pity and self-mockery are likewise combined
in the narrative poem *Soles Occidere et Redire Possunt*
which commemorates a young man killed in February
1918 :

> ' Misery,' he said, ' to have no chin,
> Nothing but brains and sex and taste
> Only omissively to sin,
> Weakly kind and cowardly chaste.
>
> But when the war is over,
> I will go to the East and plant
> Tea and rubber, and make much money.
> I will eat the black sweat of niggers
> And flagellate them with whips.

I shall be enormously myself,
Incarnate Chin.'

This may be contrasted with :

A truce to summer and beauty and the pain
Of being too consciously alive among
The things that pass and the things that remain,
(Oh, equal sadness !) the pain of being young.

Guy, in *Happily Ever After*, expresses even more
intensely than the similar Denis of *Crome Yellow*
a mood of self-disgust. Guy is described as a
' Salvationist '—' Intellectually he was a Voltairian,
emotionally a Bunyanite.' The phrase undoubtedly
describes, if summarily and incompletely, Aldous
Huxley himself at one stage of his career.

Obviously, it is still to some extent true. A man
cannot be deeply concerned about the problems of
human life without being a salvationist. He is bound
to be looking at least for his own salvation, if not
for that of others.

Huxley first began to see much of Lawrence in
1926. In him he met a salvationist more intent than
himself upon showing the world the way to heaven,
in fact a fanatical missionary. The short novel
Two or Three Graces, published in 1926, contains
what appears to be a portrait of Lawrence, drawn,
with a touch of caricature, after a few meetings.

The feeling that it was bad to neglect the physical
side of life for an excessive cultivation of the mental,
Huxley had experienced more than once before he
met Lawrence. The physically beautiful George of
Happily Ever After, the accomplished gallantry of

Ivor in *Crome Yellow*, certain experiences of Chelifer in *Those Barren Leaves*, the necessity of Gumbril to convert himself artificially into ' the Complete Man,' all indicate that Huxley was dissatisfied with intellectualism. Lawrence helped to focus that dissatisfaction into a definite doctrine.

' What Lawrence was crusading for,' says Huxley in 1931, ' was the admission by the conscious spirit of the right of the body and the instincts, not merely to a begrudged existence, but to an equal honour with itself. Man is an animal that thinks. To be a first-rate human being, a man must be both a first-rate animal and a first-rate thinker (and, incidentally, he cannot be a first-rate thinker, at any rate about human affairs, unless he is also a first-rate animal).'

Lawrence's philosophy was peculiarly adapted to attract Huxley because of its idealistic nature. Huxley is a materialist conscious all the time of a strain of idealism in the depths of his being. But he had come to distrust idealism because of its so frequent and so unpleasant distortions.

Thus, he satirizes idealistic religiosity in *Chawdron*, and idealistic art and ethics in *The Claxtons*. And in his own name somewhat heavily emphasizes his own preference for the material, the concrete over whatever is spiritual, idealistic, or mental, so that we begin to suspect an over-compensation. Very revealing in this matter are certain commentaries in his anthology *Texts and Pretexts*.

Thus, on page 7, he writes: 'I have always thought it rather degrading for an adult to believe in fairy stories.' And again :

'I prefer being sober to even the rosiest and most agreeable of intoxications. The peyotl-trances of Swinburne, for example, have always left me perfectly *compos mentis*; I do not catch the infection. Much even of Shelley's poetry is, for me, too swimmingly the coloured dream; and even when it is not dreamlike, its long-drawn imprecision is apt to flow past me, unmovingly.'

After that just criticism of the bonelessness of Shelley, it is a little surprising to find that he is quoted more often in *Texts and Pretexts* than any other author.

Again, referring to 'self is an illusion' philosophies, he comments: 'My mind has never been subtle enough to see much difference between such illusions and reality.' The touch of the sarcastic in the phrasing indicates, I think, that he is fighting against a temptation, the very alluring temptation of the illusion, which he hankers after, even in rejecting it.

Speaking of subjective idealism and Blake, he writes :

'No philosopher is quite so exciting as Blake; for none has the art of mingling such profound and important truths with such beautiful, wish-fulfilling errors. Add the finest poetry or a magnificently gnomic prose, and you have a mixture that turns the strongest heads.

However, there are also mornings after. For me, to-day is one of them. I have slept off my dose of Blake and write sober.'

It is a relief to wake sober, for evidently it was a narrow escape from the Devil and all his works. And then, on the next page :

' The religion of imagination is a dangerous faith, liable to the most deplorable corruptions. But, all the same, how lovely Mallarmé's sonnet is ! How profoundly satisfying ! '

Finally, he admits, that though he may embrace a philosophic materialism, his temperament rejects the rich, ordinary materialism of wine, women and song :

' The earthly paradise ! The earthly paradise ! With what longing, between the bars of my temperament, do I peer at its bright landscape, how voluptuously sniff at its perfumes of hay and raspberries, of honeysuckle and roast duck, of sun-warmed flesh and nectarines and the sea ! But the bars are solid ; the earthly paradise is always on the further side. Self-hindered, I cannot enter and make myself at home.'

He agrees that :

' Lived too consciously by people whose native place is on the mental plane of existence, life in the earthly paradise turns rancid and becomes strangely repulsive.'

And :

' The earthly paradise is peopled by Psyches. The intellectual Cupids can only look on from a distance and wish that their poor godheads were of another kind.'

The expressions of preference for the real, the material, the sober, as opposed to the imagined, the ideal, the intoxicated, given sometimes with a noticeable truculence, demonstrate, it seems to me, quite clearly that the foundation of Huxley's materialism is a natural idealism. It is due perhaps to his upbringing, which I have already mentioned, in part also to those years of partial blindness which cut him off from the ordinary sensual world. But that idealism is something which the mature Huxley dislikes, wants to escape from, is something which must be constantly fought.

It is very possibly this civil war which is the cause of the irritation and annoyance felt by the ordinary, confusedly idealistic reader in perusing Huxley's works. Without being able to explain how, the reader senses a truculence, an aggressiveness. The materialism is felt to be an aggressive materialism, seeking to proselytize. Which indeed it is. Huxley is eternally seeking to convert himself. For a time he succeeds, but always there are backslidings. With his intelligence he is bound to admit that it cannot be otherwise. He must remain on the intellectual plane, but nevertheless he longs for the earthly paradise. Hence his materialism is a sardonic, ironic, self-hating philosophy. And of all states of mind, such a state is most calculated to cause discomfort and distress to the ordinary reader.

How deep Huxley's own inward distress has been may be seen from such lines as :

> And yet for me who look on it, how wide
> The world of mud to which my thoughts condemn
> This loathing vision of a sunken tide !
> The ebb is mine.   Life to its lowest neap
> Withdrawn reveals that black and hideous shoal
> Where I lie stranded.   Oh deliver me
> From this defiling death !   Moon of the soul,
> Call back the tide that ran so strong and deep,
> Call back the shining jewel of the sea.

In *Do What You Will* Huxley expounds in a number of essays a philosophy of life-worship. It is a creed which should be of the highest value to hundreds living under the conditions of contemporary industrial and intellectual civilization. The primary emotion which inspired that philosophy, the first inrush of worship for instinctive life he has described in one of the finest of his poems, *The Cicadas*.

The unending vigorous chirping of the crickets at night becomes the symbol of life itself :

> I hear them sing, who in the double night
> Of clouds and branches fancied that I went
> Through my own spirit's dark discouragement,
> Deprived of inward as of outward sight ;

Who, seeking, even as here in the wild wood,
A lamp to beckon through my tangled fate,
Found only darkness and, disconsolate,
Mourned the lost purpose and the vanished good.

Now in my empty heart the crickets' shout
Re-echoing denies and still denies
With stubborn folly all my learned doubt,
In madness more than I in reason wise.

Life, life ! The word is magical. They sing,
And in my darkened soul the great sun shines ;
My fancy blossoms with remembered spring,
And all my autumns ripen on the vines.

    .   .   .   .   .   .

Clueless we go ; but I have heard thy voice,
Divine Unreason ! harping in the leaves,
And grieve no more ; for wisdom never grieves,
And thou hast taught me wisdom ; I rejoice.

An enthusiasm for whatever is splendidly human, an ironic Johnson's concern for ' the dignity of thinking beings,' has always distinguished the work of Aldous Huxley. His progression from intellectualism to the modified Lawrencian doctrine of life-worship has been inspired throughout by the desire to attain a more complete humanity than intellectualism alone could give. At the same time he has been fully aware that emotionalism alone is as incomplete as untempered intellectualism. The two must be balanced in a harmony. To achieve this harmony a native gift of style is indispensable.

' Some people,' he says, ' exist Miltonically and some Wilcoxically ; some in the style of *Figaro*,

others in that of *The Merry Widow*.' The whole of
Huxley's work says unmistakably that however his
philosophy may be criticized, it is not a mean or a
commonplace philosophy. Huxley is one of the few
people in the modern world who live Miltonically.
Though he may abandon unmodified intellectualism
as inadequate, he will never abandon the intellectual
dignity of man; he will never consent to live Wilcoxically.

He says, revealingly, in speaking of Piero della
Francesca :

> ' I am attracted to his character by his intel-
> lectual power; by his capacity for unaffectedly
> making the grand and noble gesture; by his pride
> in whatever is splendid in humanity.'

These are, it is evident, as much attributes of
Huxley's own character as they are of Piero della
Francesca's. But to display them is more difficult
for Huxley, because the modern world in which he
lives is so little sympathetic to the intellectual, the
grand and the splendidly human. Huxley's passion
for these things can often only manifest itself nega-
tively, in his criticism of the lack of them in the
contemporary world. To make the grand and noble
gesture is especially difficult. He has, I think, come
nearest to it in his play *The World of Light*.

Some future work may more continuously attain
the grand and the noble than this play does. But
whether it does so or not, and whatever changes
Huxley may make in his philosophy of life, he will,

one cannot doubt, remain faithful to these three attributes of Piero della Francesca which he so greatly
admires.

II

A Psychological Portrait

In *Proper Studies* Huxley has described in more
or less scientific terms his own type of mind. The
passages of description are somewhat scattered, and
it would, I think, be useful for the understanding of
his writing to build up from the materials given a
brief psychological portrait. This we can best do
by assembling in as continuous a narrative as possible
the essentials of his own descriptions.

'If I had to define my position,' he says, ' in
relation to Jung's system of the co-ordinates, I
should say that I was a moderately extraverted
intellectual. . . . I have no dislike or fear of external objects, and feel no objection to immersing
myself in them. . . . Intellectually I am able to
understand the doctrine, for example, of the
Platonic theory of ideas ; but I am unable to discover in myself any intimate reason for believing
it. . . . Some souls are *naturaliter Christianae* :
others are congenitally materialistic. Mine belongs
to the latter category. I understand the materialist interpretation of inward life. But the introvert Procrustes, who would chop and trim the
objective world in order that it may fit the bed

he has prepared for it in his mind, seems to me a monster.'

' Certain types of extreme extravert are no less incomprehensible to me than the introvert. The really sociable man, who is only himself when he is in company, is to me a very mysterious figure. That people should be able to live without privacy and solitude strikes me as extraordinary. And how repulsive, how incomprehensible I find the philosophy which is the rationalization of these people's outward-looking passion for their fellows!'

' Another type of pronounced extravert, whose outlook on life I find it impossible to understand except theoretically, is the type of man who lives for sensations rather than for ideas or emotions. For these people, the pure sensation is so delightful, and seems in its intensity so significant, that the cultivation of sensations is a completely satisfying end in itself. . . . Oscar Wilde's is a typical extravert-sensationalist's philosophy. I understand what he writes, but can discover no personal reason in myself for accepting his major premisses. Indeed, when I read a book by Wilde, I feel the most intimate personal reasons for rejecting them.'

' My own thinking is predominantly extraverted ; but I have a great dislike of practical activity. I am interested in the outside world, but only intellectually, not practically. My ambition and my pleasure are to understand, not to act : and when action becomes necessary, I grudge the time I must devote to doing things in a world which I desire only intellectually to comprehend.'

' To me the craftsman-ideal is simply a nightmare. I should go mad or commit suicide if I were compelled to waste my time (for in my eyes it would be a waste) making my own boots and buttons, growing my own vegetables, building my own house.'

' It is extremely difficult for a person having one type of mind to understand the workings of a mind of the opposite type. I am myself a very imperfect visualizer. By making an effort of will, I am able to conjure up before my mind's eye images of a moderate clarity and vividness. But images do not come to me spontaneously. I think normally in terms of words which represent an analysis of the things I am thinking of. Sometimes, even, it seems to me that I think directly in terms of that analysis without employing words at all. But of this I cannot be certain. In any case when I wish to form a mental image, I do so piecemeal, by putting together the analysis of the thing I want to see, and translating it deliberately into visual terms. When I have to calculate, I do so abstractly, without seeing the digits or representing them to myself as having any particular position in space.'

' I am ordinarily of a very calm and even phlegmatic temperament,' he says in a *Sunday Referee* article on the effects of influenza. ' But fever changed all this. External sensations which were normally agreeable or indifferent became unbearably acute. I had the impression that every touch, every sight and sound, was something that rasped upon my nerves with innumerable fine bristling points.

'I cannot describe what happened better than by saying that, at ordinary times, my sensations are smooth and cool, that they touch me, so to speak, with surfaces of polished metal or satin; but that, when the fever was on me, they became harsh and hairy and that their touch was like that of a door-mat.'

In this portrait we might include a passage from *Point Counter Point* which shows that Huxley is able to put the case against himself better than any outsider could.

Philip Quarles, a character created in Huxley's own image, is reflecting on himself:

'But this question of identity was precisely one of Philip's chronic problems. It was so easy for him to be almost anybody, theoretically and with his intelligence. He had such power of assimilation, that he was often in danger of being unable to distinguish the assimilator from the assimilated, of not knowing among the multiplicity of his rôles who was the actor. . . . He had been a cynic and also a mystic, a humanitarian and also a contemptuous misanthrope; he had tried to live the life of detached and stoical reason, and another time he had aspired to the unreasonableness of natural and uncivilized existence. The choice of moulds

depended at any given moment on the books he
was reading, the people he was associating with.

' But the essential liquidness that flowed where it
would, the cool indifferent flux of intellectual
curiosity—that persisted and to that his loyalty
was due. . . . Against the pyrrhonian suspense of
judgment and the stoical imperturbability he had
often rebelled. But had the rebellion ever been
really serious? . . . always, whatever he might do,
he knew quite well in the secret depths of his being
that he wasn't a Catholic, or a strenuous liver, or a
mystic or a noble savage. And although he sometimes nostalgically wished he were one or other of
these things, or all of them at once, he was always
secretly glad to be none of them and at liberty,
even though his liberty was in a strange paradoxical
way a handicap and a confinement to his spirit.'

Chapter 3

THE NOVELS

But then I never pretended to be a congenital novelist.
Philip Quarles in *Point Counter Point*.

I

Point Counter Point

UNLESS a novelist is content with plain story-telling, experiment is indispensable. Without it, one has not the heart to go on. Actually very few novelists of importance have ever been satisfied simply to tell a story. By itself the story belongs to the primitive level of literature, corresponding with the primitive part of man's psychology, and is, like that, regrettable perhaps, but inevitable.

No one has discussed this regrettable necessity with more penetration than Mr. E. M. Forster in his *Aspects of the Novel*. The essence of the story as he sees it is time—the naked tape-worm of time which ties incident to incident. All that the story does is to answer the question ' And then . . . and then ? '

Daily life is full of time, of events happening one after another. But ' there seems something else in life besides time, something which may conveniently be called " value." '

Looking back on one's life, one is conscious not of an evenly spaced sequence of events, but of days that were worth more than years, of hours that weighed more than days. Moments of ecstasy shine out like candles in a dark church; but candles which are scattered about irregularly over the whole rambling edifice of one's life, rather than arranged in orderly procession.

These moments of ecstasy, these irregularly scattered candles are what Mr. Forster means by 'value.' And in the process of writing a novel, one longs to construct it entirely of value. The high-lights, the golden candles are so delightful, the flat, necessary narrative so exasperating. One aches to have done with it, if possible to cut it out altogether.

'What the story does,' says Mr. Forster, 'is to narrate the life in time. And what the entire novel does—if it is a good novel—is to include the life by values as well.' But, he adds, with perhaps unjustified pessimism, ' The time-sequence cannot be destroyed without carrying in its ruin all that should have taken its place : the novel that would express values only becomes unintelligible and therefore valueless.'

Now that is the problem facing the novelist who is not content with mere story-telling : to have all value and no time. Or at least the minimum of time and the maximum of value—say ten per cent. of one and ninety of the other. Mr. Forster mentions Emily Brontë, Sterne, Proust and Gertrude Stein as novelists who have attempted either to limit time in fiction or abolish it altogether. He might also have mentioned Virginia Woolf, Joyce and Huxley.

In his *Point Counter Point* Huxley has made one of the most successful efforts to express the life of values with the least possible dilution of time that exists in English. Of his five novels it is undoubtedly the best. He has himself expressed a preference for it as being ' the most complete and the most solid.' It may be described as having done for English fiction what André Gide's *Les Faux-Monnayeurs* did for French, though to my mind it is a nobler and a more passionate work than Gide's.

Huxley's way of reducing the amount of time as contrasted with value, that is, his way of getting rid of the story, or overthrowing the tyranny of the plot, is to replace it with *music*.

The absence of plot does not mean that there is no action. There is a good deal of violent action. Webley, the politician, is murdered, Spandrell, the conscience-ridden intellectual turned murderer, gets killed. The child Phil dies of meningitis. Several women become the mistresses of several men. And so on. (It is probably the greater degree of action in *Point Counter Point* which is one of the reasons for its having a greater solidity than Huxley's other novels.) But the distinguishing character of these events, as compared with the events in novels with a plot, is that nothing is ever brought to a final, logical conclusion. At no point in the book, not even at the end, can you lean back and, sighing with satisfaction, dream of happiness ever after for your favourite character. Nothing is ever deliberately foreordained. The connection between the characters is not a plot connection. It is merely that of life, that they happen to know one another. The form of the book, the pattern, is obtained by weaving together, generally with ironic effect, variations on one or two themes which the different sets of characters represent. This is what I mean by *music* in the place of story or plot.

Besides demonstrating this idea concretely in *Point Counter Point*, Huxley discusses it abstractly in the same book through his novelist hero Philip Quarles.

' The musicalization of fiction,' the latter writes in his notebook. ' Not in the symbolist way, by subordinating sense to sound. . . . But on a large scale, in the construction. Meditate on Beethoven. The changes of mood, the abrupt transitions. (Majesty alternating with a joke, for example, in the first movement of the B flat major quartet. Comedy suddenly hinting at prodigious and tragic solemnities in the scherzo of the C sharp minor quartet.) More interesting still the modulations, not merely from one key to another, but from mood to mood. A theme is stated, then developed, pushed out of shape, imperceptibly deformed, until, though still recognizably the same, it has become quite different. In sets of variations the process is carried a step further. Those incredible Diabelli variations, for example. The whole range of thought and feeling, yet all in organic relation to a ridiculous little waltz tune. Get this into a novel. How ? The abrupt transitions are easy enough. All you need is a sufficiency of characters and parallel, contrapuntal plots.

While Jones is murdering a wife, Smith is wheeling
the perambulator in the park. You alternate the
themes. More interesting, the modulations and
variations are also more difficult. A novelist
modulates by reduplicating situations and characters. He shows several people falling in love,
or dying, or praying in different ways—dissimilars
solving the same problem. Or, *vice versa*, similar
people confronted with dissimilar problems. In
this way you can modulate through all the aspects
of your theme, you can write variations in any
number of different moods. Another way : The
novelist can assume the god-like creative privilege
and simply elect to consider the events of the story
in their various aspects—emotional, economic,
religious, metaphysical, etc. He will modulate
from one to the other—as from the aesthetic to
the physico-chemical aspect of things, from the
religious to the physiological or financial.'

This paragraph contains packed into it some of
the most interesting and stimulating ideas on the
craft of the novel that have yet been suggested by
any one. Here Huxley inspires one with the enthusiastic conviction that to write a novel is the easiest
and most delightful thing in the world ; he brings
fresh interest into a problem that one is apt to regard
as chewed to the bone. And this, I think, indicates
what good criticism it is. Perhaps one of the most
fruitful and immediately valuable uses of criticism
is to stimulate the creative imagination to fresh efforts.

The best of Pater's writings have this quality. An imaginative writer feeling his faculties dulled, his imagination devoid of life, of ideas, has only to read the essay on ' Style,' or ' The School of Giorgione,' or that on Winckelmann, to find his imagination again warming to invention, to feel once more that his medium still offers the most fascinating possibilities.

I shall quote more of the critical passages in *Point Counter Point*, but for the present let us consider the musicalization of fiction.

It is not easy to see exactly how fiction could imitate the abrupt transitions of music. The use of a multitude of characters and parallel plots would not really do it, because the reader would separate out in his mind the stories which the author had been at such pains to weave together. The alternation of Jones murdering his wife and Smith wheeling the perambulator would not produce the effect desired ; it would merely cause the fabric to fall to pieces. The scenes in which Jones appeared would run together ; similarly with the Smith scenes. They would inevitably tend to combine in this way rather than in the criss-cross weave which the device is intended to produce. The reasons are, I think, that fiction is too diffuse, and does not move as swiftly as music. Huxley, questioned on this point, agreed that the novelist can never really achieve the striking, abrupt transitions of music, partly for the reasons just given, and also, he suggested, because fiction is not so symbolic as music.

The parallel plot idea is not used in *Point Counter*

Point, though there is something on related lines in Chapter XI with its alternations of the chatter over the dinner table in Sbisa's restaurant, and the scientific conversation of Lord Edward Tantamount and Illidge. There are also other examples.

The effect of sudden changes of mood would naturally be ironical. If the novel could be made to move swiftly enough to impress the succeeding moods sharply upon the reader, it would be possible to produce a novel acutely ironical in total effect, though devoid of irony in the detail. The irony would be in the construction.

Huxley has done this not by the use of sudden transitions—a difficult and perhaps impossible method —but by his variations and modulations on a theme. He has used both the ways suggested by Philip Quarles: showing dissimilars solving the same problem; and modulating from one aspect of an event to another. This latter trick is particularly characteristic of Huxley's writing. He excels in the production of ironical effects obtained by juxtaposing learned scientific, literary or historical knowledge with some ordinary, immediate physical sensation or fact. His books abound in examples of it, and he has discussed it theoretically in *Music at Night* (p. 40).

The theme of *Point Counter Point* is announced in the quotation from Fulke Greville on the page following the title-page, particularly in the last couplet:

> *What meaneth nature by these diverse laws,*
> *Passion and reason, self-division's cause?*

The self-division of reasoning beings is the subject of the book.

The theme is first stated in terms of Marjorie Carling, a rather banal young woman, heavily and earnestly cultured, and Walter Bidlake, a young man intellectually idealistic, but emotionally corporeal.

Marjorie is Walter's mistress.

The book begins :

'"You won't be late?" There was anxiety in Marjorie Carling's voice, there was something like entreaty.

"No, I won't be late," said Walter, unhappily and guiltily certain that he would be.'

Perhaps a rather sloppy, formless dive into the heart of things. It is the kind of opening which schools of journalism might teach as a selling line. It arrests the reader's attention. He at once is inter ested to know more of the obviously unhappy relations between Marjorie and the potential loiterer. His interest grows when half-way down the page he discovers that ' She had left her husband to live with Walter Bidlake.' Undoubtedly, it is immediately effective, intriguing. Like a newspaper serial, it ' grips.'

But to be ' gripped' by Huxley is a distressing experience. We wish he would not do it. We feel the same kind of embarrassment, of vexation at gratuitous stupidity as the father of a naturally well-behaved child who suddenly makes a deliberate, yet slightly inefficient effort to be naughty.

It is possible to regard the opening page of *Point*

Counter Point for these reasons as regrettable. On the other hand we may consider the novelette opening as being deliberately chosen as the most appropriate key to express the banality of Marjorie Carling's character, rather in the same way as Gide first thought of opening *Les Faux-Monnayeurs* in a café: ' La banalité même du lieu m'a tenté ' (*Journal des Faux-Monnayeurs*, p. 18). It is, I admit, possible that this ' gripping ' first page was deliberate ; but the fact that the reader is left in two minds about whether the author is demonstrating his skill, or suffering from fatigue, appears to me to show that the deliberate use of banality is not deliberate enough.

Fortunately, Huxley relaxes his ' grip ' after a page or so, and describes in ten superb pages the tortures of remorse, desire and the death of desire in clear, sinewy prose which puts an unfaltering line round every twist and wrinkle of passion. From then on the novel slowly unfolds itself with a luxuriant assurance. Scene follows scene without hesitation. No doubts—or none left visible. Never a flagging of interest, everything working to a magnificent climax and then a dying fall in two pages of quiet irony.

*   *   *

I mentioned above the ironic effects which Huxley gets by juxtaposing learned knowledge with human fact. It would be well to deal with that point now.

An example from *Point Counter Point* (p. 2) :

' Six months from now her baby would be born. Something that had been a single cell, a cluster of

cells, a little sac of tissue, a kind of worm, a potential
fish with gills, stirred in her womb and would one
day become a man—a grown man, suffering and
enjoying, loving and hating, thinking, remember-
ing, imagining.'

Or again (p. 205) :

' A cell had multiplied itself and become a worm,
the worm had become a fish, the fish was turning
into the fœtus of a mammal. Marjorie felt sick and
tired. Fifteen years hence a boy would be con-
firmed. Enormous in his robes, like a full-rigged
ship, the Bishop would say : " Do ye here in the
presence of God, and of this congregation, renew the
solemn promise and vow that was made in your
name at your Baptism ? " And the ex-fish would
answer with passionate conviction : " I do." '

It is common to describe Huxley's novels as
witty. But the humour of these and many similar
passages does not proceed from wit. The fun is not
in the least verbal. The prose is devoid of glitter ;
it is bare, scientific text-book prose. The humour
arises from the violent, grotesque contrast, from the
swift revelation of the disparity between man's
physical origin and his prodigious emotional and
religious claims. Such passages as I have quoted are
moments of high comedy in works essentially tragic.
It is a kind of comedy possible only in a society highly
civilized, as we at present measure civilization, and
extremely self-conscious. Further, it is a kind of
comedy which may, in time, become completely

unfunny. We laugh now at the ex-fish saying ' I do,' because we are still living in the shadow of the conflict between science and religion which Darwin started. Let us suppose, for the moment, that we are all practising agnostics—we base our lives on lack of faith and the assumption that the scientific view of the world is correct—nevertheless, the religion which was important to our fathers and grandfathers still casts its shadow over us, and we are so conditioned that attacks on the once sacrosanct faith still cause an emotional tremor, a shock which usually expresses itself, owing to our agnosticism, as a laugh. This effect is also due to the fact that the scientific knowledge we all theoretically *know* has by no means been absorbed into our psychological systems. We all *know* that the human embryo passes through a fish stage in the womb—that is to say we have once or twice read statements to that effect—but this knowledge does not enter into our daily life. It is something on the far fringe, in the distant Polar regions of our consciousness. Thus A, deciding whether he shall or shall not marry B, does not take into account the fact that he is an ex-fish. That he was once a kind of worm does not determine his acceptance of a post in Nigeria. Only his thoughts and feelings as a completed human being are important in these decisions. But a time may come when every one will be fully aware that he or she was once a potential fish with gills—as fully aware of this fact as we are now that we have arms and legs, bones and blood. If that should ever be so, a statement that ' the ex-fish would

answer with passionate conviction, "I do!"'' will
cease to be funny, just as it would not be funny to
write, 'The boy, consisting of bones, tissue and
blood, answered, "I do!"'

This combination of scientific knowledge with
human experience is one of the methods of writing
variations on a theme suggested in Philip Quarles's
notebook. The two ironical passages from *Point
Counter Point* so far quoted are examples of modulating
from the emotional to the scientific aspect of an event,
and from the scientific to the religious aspect.

In several interesting passages opening up fascinating, if darkly shadowed philosophical vistas, Huxley
gives a simultaneously scientific and aesthetic account
of a concert. The irony now is not sufficiently close
to the human to raise a laugh. This time it provokes
perplexing and perhaps unanswerable questions.
Thus :

'And the great Pongileoni glueily kissed his
flute. He blew across the mouth hole and a
cylindrical air column vibrated ; Bach's medita-
tions filled the Roman quadrangle. In the opening
largo John Sebastian had, with the help of Pongileoni's snout and the air column, made a statement : There are grand things in the world, noble
things ; there are men born kingly ; there are real
conquerors, intrinsic lords of the earth.'

Or again :

'In the human fugue there are eighteen hundred
million parts. The resultant noise means some-

thing perhaps to the statistician, nothing to the
artist. It is only by considering one or two parts
at a time that the artist can understand anything.
Here, for example, is one particular part ; and John
Sebastian puts the case. The Rondeau begins,
exquisitely and simply melodious, almost a folk-
song. It is a young girl singing to herself of love,
in solitude, tenderly mournful. A young girl
singing among the hills, with the clouds drifting
overhead. But solitary as one of the floating clouds,
a poet had been listening to her song. The thoughts
that it provoked in him are the Sarabande that
follows the Rondeau. His is a slow and lovely
meditation on the beauty (in spite of squalor and
stupidity), the profound goodness (in spite of all
the evil), the oneness (in spite of such bewildering
diversity) of the world. It is a beauty, a goodness,
a unity that no intellectual research can discover,
that analysis dispels, but of whose reality the spirit
is from time to time suddenly and overwhelmingly
convinced. A girl singing to herself under the
clouds suffices to create the certitude. Even a fine
morning is enough. Is it illusion or the revelation
of profoundest truth ? Who knows ? Pongileoni
blew, the fiddlers drew their rosined horsehair
across the stretched intestines of lambs ; through
the long Sarabande the poet slowly meditated his
lovely and consoling certitude.'

The certitude may be a revelation of absolute truth,
or it may be merely a result of momentary changes in

the body's chemistry. We can never know. An ironical outlook is forced upon all who are sufficiently aware of science and human emotion at the same time. ' We live in a world of *non sequiturs*. . . . Our life is spent first in one water-tight compartment of experience, then in another. The artist can, if he so desires, break down the bulkheads between the compartments and so give us a simultaneous view of two or more of them at a time. So seen reality looks exceedingly queer. Which is how the ironist and the perplexed questioner desire it to look.'

Increasingly as one reads Huxley with attention, it becomes clear that his art is ironical through and through. So far we have only looked at one of the ways in which this irony is expressed. It is time to get back to our analysis of the musical construction of *Point Counter Point*. We can note the other kinds of irony as we go along.

* * *

Walter Bidlake and Marjorie Carling are not very interesting characters. They are the first simple statement of the theme, the ' ridiculous little waltz tune ' of Huxley's Diabelli variations. And that theme we must bear in mind is :

' Passion and reason, self-division's cause.'

As the book progresses Marjorie develops a capacity for religion which makes her a little less banal than when we first meet her. But Walter hardly develops at all. From the beginning his self-division is acute : ' His love for Lucy was mad and

shameful, but Marjorie was bloodless and half-dead.'
The conflict is only solved by abandoning Marjorie
and making Lucy, the calculating siren who takes
her pleasure like a man, his mistress. But before
long Lucy goes abroad and leaves Walter, supperless,
and 'lying on the bed, his face buried in the pillows,'
with a Marjorie who finds God the perfect substitute
for an unfaithful lover. After that we hear no more
of Walter. No nicely rounded fate is provided for
him. He was the simple first statement of the theme
which has now developed into variations of vast
complexity. The melodic phrase which he represented is no longer required. But there is no feeling
of a sudden gap in the pattern, because meanwhile,
as the book progresses, two characters—Denis Burlap
and Beatrice Gilray—have been brought into the
design, and they take up the place left empty by
Walter and Marjorie. They are a restatement of the
theme represented by the latter. At the same time
they are a distinct variation on it, for while Walter
and Marjorie were seen sympathetically, Burlap and
Beatrice are seen satirically ; they live with the force
of the author's dislike, not with that of his compassion.

We may, if we choose, regard Walter as in some
respects a portrait of certain aspects of Huxley as a
young man. Walter's idealism, his endeavour to
make life conform to literature and philosophy, may
well have been typical of the young Huxley as they
are of many young men of talent. But it is not very
profitable to pursue this line of enquiry. Inevitably

the characters of every novelist are only personifica-
tions of himself ; that is to say of himself in the widest
sense, including past as well as present, and including
too all those latent desires, powers and impulses
which he has perhaps often dreamed over but never
developed or fulfilled in his personal life. Often a
character is simply the imaginative projection of
hidden latencies. Many a shy scholar is a man of
action on paper. These make good historians or
novelists of violence. Such were Kinglake, D. H.
Lawrence and Lytton Strachey. All a writer's knowledge and experience is, in reality, like that of any one
else, only knowledge and experience of himself.
And that is his only material for constructing characters and situations. A part of himself, as he is, as
he was, might have been or may still be, goes into
every one of his personages. And thus they all of
necessity lead back to the author; but to look at them
in this way is to use them as material for biography,
rather than for literary criticism.

Walter Bidlake's self-division is expressed in his
social relationships as well as in his personal ones.
The theme is restated in another key, in terms of
bourgeois and proletariat.

Walter's political opinions are advanced. In the
Underground, on his way to see Lucy Tantamount,
he reads with pleasure in his evening paper that the
Liberal-Labour Government's Bill for the national-
ization of the mines has passed its first reading. The
newspaper's leading article, violently attacking the
measure, ' evoked in him a stimulating enthusiasm

for all that it assailed, a delightful hatred for Capitalists and Reactionaries.'

Then :

'. . . a wizened little man with a red handkerchief round his neck took the seat next to him.
The stink of the old man's pipe was so suffocating
that Walter looked up the car to see if there was
not another vacant seat. . . .

" One should be loyal to one's tastes and instincts," Philip Quarles used to say. " What's the
good of a philosophy with a major premiss that
isn't the rationalization of your feelings?" . . . A
whiff of stale sweat came up with the nicotine fumes
to Walter's nostrils. . . . The little old man leaned
forward and spat, cautiously and perpendicularly,
between his feet. With the heel of his boot he
spread the gob over the floor. Walter looked
away ; he wished that he could personally like
the oppressed. . . . One should be loyal to one's
tastes and instincts. But one's tastes and instincts
were accidents. There were eternal principles.
But if the axiomatic principles didn't happen to
be your personal major premiss . . .?'

Then he remembers the occasion when as a boy he
was taken to visit a sick under-gardener, and how
disgust at the sick-room smell routed pity. The
debate finds a new example.

And then :

' Honour, fidelity—these were good things. But
the personal major premiss of his present philosophy

was that Lucy Tantamount was the most beautiful, the most desirable . . .'

So the struggle goes on. His political opinions are advanced, but he dislikes the working-classes; he admires honour and fidelity but he cannot give up Lucy. ' Passion and reason, self-division's cause.' The wizened little man with the red handkerchief round his neck is the first statement of a new theme in *Point Counter Point*, a theme new also to all Huxley's fiction : that is, the proletariat. Except for a brief, brilliantly managed passage in *Antic Hay* the working-classes have never before intruded into the warm, well-lit world of Huxley's fiction. And that brief strophe and anti-strophe in *Antic Hay* merely demonstrated an uneasy awareness of the vast grey crowds outside the drawing-room windows. It was a moment of alarm, or wonder ; not one of interest.

Huxley has again and again confessed, in his novels, essays, and in conversation, that he is acutely aware of feeling a foreigner among many sections of his own countrymen. And nowhere is he more foreign than among the poor, the working-class. ' Those of us who have lived in tolerable economic security are foreigners among our poorer compatriots. Whether we like it or no, we belong to a different nationality ' (*Sunday Referee*, 17 December 1933). Wisely he has seldom attempted to describe the life of these foreigners among his own compatriots.

But in *Point Counter Point* he has abandoned prudence, perhaps owing to the influence of Lawrence,

or perhaps because he felt the need to extend the range
of his art, and has produced in Illidge, the proletarian
scientist, Communist and political murderer, a character of exceptional interest. Even now, however,
Huxley has had to make one concession to his domin-
ating interests : his proletarian has to be a scientist.
He could not be a tram-driver, or a greengrocer,
because Huxley knows so little about the lives of
tram-drivers and greengrocers. But science is the
same with or without aspirates. Boyle's Law is
indifferent to Oxonian baa-ings or Cockney diph-
thongs. Hence Huxley can create a working-class
scientist if not a tram-driver.

Illidge too is a self-divided character. His Communism conflicts with his science, as well as with his
natural human feelings. The outcome is political
murder. Illidge provides, incidentally, the text for a
rapid notation and criticism of the peculiar claim of
Communists that their political and historical theory
is *scientific*.

Spandrell, Illidge's companion murderer, remarks :

> ' You can't be a true Communist without being a
> mechanist. You've got to believe that the only
> fundamental realities are space, time and mass. . . .
> Poor Illidge ! He's sadly worried by Einstein and
> Eddington. . . . He's a scientist, but his principles
> make him fight against any scientific theory that's
> less than fifty years old.'

Nothing is, indeed, more remarkable than the naïf
way in which Communist writers use the epithet

' scientific.' Any one who has ever read Communist periodicals or pamphlets will recall the frequent appeal which is made to this magic word. Communism, they declare, is ' scientific,' and in saying this, Communist writers obviously feel that they are advancing the most striking and novel argument, to which the reader will at once yield his assent. But the alleged ' scientific ' quality of Communism is precisely what seems most doubtful. In the first place, it is difficult to see how any interpretation of history—the material of which is imponderable human nature— can ever be scientific. Kings, Parliaments and people are alike inaccessible to the laboratory. And in the second place, the science that Marx and Engels knew was nineteenth-century materialism. This is the science to which contemporary Communist writers still refer. To be a Communist, as Huxley says, means that you are committed to nineteenth-century materialism. Aware of this, those who no longer accept materialism as the last word will not so easily be charmed into agreement by the Communist emphasis upon the ' scientific ' character of the faith.[1]

[1] I find an excellent example of this assumption that Communism is scientific in the most exact sense in *The Left Review*, November 1934. Mr. Edgell Rickword, reviewing Mr. G. B. Shaw's *Prefaces*, says : ' He speaks of Russia as being ruled by a hierarchy like that of the Catholic Church, where the Communist Manifesto has " scriptural authority." (Does the bridge-builder give " scriptural authority " to the first book of Euclid, because he finds that things do happen like that ?) ' The sentence in parentheses says, in effect : Communism is to society as Euclid is to engineering. Which, as Euclid would say, is absurd.

'Passion and reason . . .' Spandrell continues his description of Illidge :

'I can give you examples of his practical inconsistencies. I discovered . . . that Illidge has the most touching sense of family loyalty. He keeps his mother, he pays for his younger brother's education, he gave his sister fifty pounds when she married. . . . Theoretically he sees no distinction between his mother and any other aged female. He knows that, in a properly organized society, she'd be put into the lethal chamber because of her arthritis. In spite of which he sends her I don't know how much a week to enable her to drag on a useless existence.'

Spandrell finds the spectacle of Illidge's inconsistencies 'exquisitely comic.' Huxley finds them ironic—and that means sometimes comic, and sometimes tragic. The entire human situation, properly speaking, is ironical. Irony is a warmer, more human way than Pascal's of regarding the infinite spaces. Instead of terror, the ironist's response is a smile and a shake of the head.

We have now examined the first statement of the 'self-division' theme of *Point Counter Point*—Walter Bidlake—and one variation on it—Illidge. Walter's self-division is of the commonest kind, a simple conflict in sexual relations. Illidge's is further from the primary impulses, and being mainly intellectual, is less common. He represents a modulation to the minor from the major key of Walter's elementary inconsistencies.

In the same way we could trace variations on the theme in certain other characters. Burlap, for instance, trying to make himself believe in the spiritual life while keeping a cool eye on his investments. He is the hypocrite, the man who is unconscious of his self-division. Sidney Quarles, a prey to the conflicts of ambition and indolence ; Spandrell, hating his mother because he once loved her so much ; and Elinor Quarles, Philip's wife, with her deliberate effort to love Everard Webley fighting against her instinctive revulsion.

In following the working-out of this theme, we must not, naturally, insist too heavily upon it. It would be a mistake to seek in every character an illustration of the main theme. There are subsidiary ones. And also, it is important to note, there is what we may call a counter-theme.

Opposed to the idea of self-division is the idea of wholeness.

' " It's time," ' says Mark Rampion, ' " It's time there was a revolt in favour of life and wholeness." '

This is the answering theme to 'Passion and reason, self-division's cause.' It is from the interweaving of the two themes that the counterpoint of *ideas* in the novel is built up, parallel to the counterpoint of *form*. The first hint of the counter-theme is on page 18, when Walter Bidlake recalls Philip Quarles's remark : ' " One should be loyal to one's tastes and instincts." '

The principal exponent of wholeness is Mark Rampion, a character based upon the life and ideas of D. H. Lawrence.[1]

He and his wife are the only really unified man and woman among a crowd of self-divided personalities. Philip Quarles, to some extent a portrait of Aldous Huxley himself, has achieved a kind of wholeness, but by cutting away, rather than by building in. He has tried to cut out every part of himself that is not of the reason, the speculating intellect. In his desire for freedom he has suppressed all natural piety, all instinctive, irrational life, only to find that by so doing he has desiccated the very intelligence for whose sake he performed these mutilations. Uneasily he becomes aware of the fact that his wholeness is only a precarious, superficial wholeness ; that a man is always more than his intelligence, and that the roots of the lopped-off instincts and emotions always remain, perhaps to fester unseen.

In Rampion's phrase, Philip Quarles is a ' barbarian of the intellect.' Rampion's ideal man is William Blake. ' Civilization,' says Rampion, ' is harmony and completeness. Reason, feeling, instinct, the life of the body—Blake managed to include and har-

---

[1] Lawrence's reaction to Rampion was one of defensive contempt. '. . . your Rampion,' he writes in a letter to Aldous Huxley, ' is the most boring character in the book—a gas-bag. Your attempt at intellectual sympathy !—It's all rather disgusting, and I feel like a badger that has its hole on Wimbledon Common, and trying not to be caught.' (*The Letters of D. H. Lawrence*, p. 758. Edited by Aldous Huxley. Heinemann, 1932.)

monize everything. Barbarism is being lop-sided.
You can be a barbarian of the intellect as well as of
the body. A barbarian of the soul and feelings as well
as of sensuality. Christianity made us barbarians of
the soul, and now science is making us barbarians of
the intellect. Blake was the last civilized man.'

Thus the wholeness which Rachel Quarles has
achieved through Christianity is not, in Rampion's
eyes, a genuine wholeness for a civilized person. She
is suffering from what he calls ' Jesus's disease.' The
general disease of modern man is ' Jesus's disease
and Newton's disease and Henry Ford's disease.'
Between them the Christian, the scientist and the big-
business man have sucked the life out of the contemporary man.

Rampion's wholeness is the envy of Philip Quarles.

' After a few hours in Rampion's company he
really believed in noble savagery ; he felt convinced
that the proudly conscious intellect ought to humble
itself a little and admit the claims of the heart,
aye, and of the bowels, the loins, and the bones
and skin and muscles to a fair share of life. . . .
Rampion was the proof of his own theories. " If
I could capture something of his secret ! " Philip
sighed to himself.'

In *Music at Night* (page 21) Huxley refers to the
fact that the play which was made out of *Point
Counter Point* omitted most of the ' counter ' which
was intended to temper the harshness of the ' points.'

Under the heading of ' counter ' come many of

the scenes devoted to the discussion of this balancing-theme of ' wholeness.'

Chapter XVI, for example, in any novel with a strict plot would be a digression. All it does is to give a dramatic exposition of Rampion's ideas. Even in a plotless novel like *Point Counter Point*, the chapter might become an excrescence, were it not handled so skilfully. But the dialogue in this chapter (it is almost all dialogue) is not simply talk distributed among labelled voices, as it sometimes is in *Crome Yellow*. Besides expressing certain principles of living, the dialogue reveals the personal relationship between Rampion, the exponent of physical and spiritual wholeness, and Burlap, the hypocritical, comfortably-off expert on Lady Poverty. The slightly amused contempt of Rampion for Burlap and the latter's deliberate effort at sympathy for a man he can never really understand, are brought out in the way each approaches the same ideas. Then, in the last few lines of the chapter, Huxley gets one of those ironic effects which seem at first glance, so naturally do they arise, to be merely transcriptions of obvious reality.

Burlap is writing a life of St. Francis of Assisi. ' Oh Poverty, Poverty, beautiful Lady Poverty! . . .' he writes.

Then :

> ' " I want to ask your advice about some gramophone shares I've got," said Beatrice. " They've been rising so violently."

" Gramophones ! " said Burlap. " Ah ! . . ."
He advised.'

A great deal of the ' counter ' in the novel relates
closely to Huxley and his personal development.
The problems involved are treated also in his essays
and it will be more convenient to deal with them in
that connection. For the present it is sufficient to
note that this ' counter,' though detachable for critical
examination, is firmly written into the composition of
the book. It is as much a part of the whole complex
musical structure as the murder of Everard Webley,
or the love affairs of Walter Bidlake. We do not, in
reading the ' counter ' parts of the novel, experience
any tedium. There is no anxiety to get to the next
'point.' The digressions are not felt as such. Nothing
breaks the strong, compelling pattern of the design.
This is Huxley's great achievement : to have
created a new form for the novel, a form which is
able to absorb so much digressive material and yet
never, as it were, lose speed. The sense of richness,
of abundance of life, which is one of the strongest
impressions left by *Point Counter Point*, is due to this
incorporation of so much varied, and (apparently)
irrelevant material. Without it the novel would
seem, as Huxley found the play, ' hard and brutal.'
So rich is *Point Counter Point* in ideas and so interesting are these ideas that one is tempted to discuss
them as though they existed independently, and to
forget that for the moment at least they should be
considered only as elements in a work of fiction.

Their part in the novel, their contribution to the total effect, is all that should concern us now, not their ultimate truth. And since we shall find most of them expounded elsewhere in Huxley's work, we can easily leave ultimate truth on one side for the time being.

The very actuality of some novels of ideas has rendered them merely academic to later generations. To be appropriate to one's age is well enough, but to be only appropriate is to write at the temperature of journalism rather than of literature. Peacock, learned and high-spirited though he may be, suffers from this defect. One cannot find his lukewarm satire on the economist, poet, and other intellectuals gathered at Crotchet Castle more than mildly amusing. Adam Smith, Scotch reviewers, Mechanics' Institutes and the ' march of mind ' are no longer matters of passionate fashionable concern. And Peacock does not really care about them enough to make us care. He is only contemptuous in a mild, gentlemanly way. And so we cannot be more than mildly and gentlemanly amused at his ' Steam Intellect Society,' his Mr. Macquedy, Mr. Skionar, Mr. Trillo, Mr. Firedamp and Mr. Henbane, whose names are ridiculous without being comic. In exactly the same way Freud, cubist painting, Communism among the intelligentsia and the theory of Relativity will in themselves be of as little interest to the future as nineteenth-century excitements are to us. Characters labelled ' Mr. Bolshy,' ' Mr. Ego,' ' Mr. Fourth-dimension ' would not simply on that account be particularly funny to the readers of A.D. 2000. And if Huxley had written merely in this Peacockian manner, his books would be designed to a future on high and dusty shelves. But his great superiority over Peacock (with whom *Crome Yellow* and *Those Barren Leaves* certainly show affinities) is his interest in character. Peacock, a fine classical scholar, was a man of wide reading, but of narrow sympathies. Incapable of absorption in the lives of others, even in the scientific 'Fabre-among-the-coleoptera' way of Aldous Huxley, he is not interested in character, and is unable to create anything but marionettes. Huxley has gone far beyond anything Peacock could do. His satire of fashionable ideas is far sharper, because he sees them, not as mere floating conceptions which can be symbolized by a farcical name, but as something incorporated into the lives of men and women. He can satirize the modern religious hypocrite because he has seen and observed Burlap with a close and fascinated watchfulness. Where Peacock would have called his comfortably-off hypocrite 'Mr. Soulful-Moneybags,' thus creating nothing but a puppet, Huxley uses his imagination and adopts an odd and slightly comic word as a name which we at once joyfully accept. Burlap—nothing could better express the sweet, sticky emotionalism in which the man excels. It is perfect. And thus with all Huxley's names for his characters. They are at once possible, appropriate and, where necessary, satirical. Sometimes, as with Mr. Mercaptan of *Antic Hay*, their discovery ('The mercaptans are colourless fluids having a strong, repulsive, garlic odour'—Webster) is pure genius.

Philip Quarles writes of the novel of ideas :

'The character of each personage must be implied, as far as possible, in the ideas of which he is the mouthpiece. In so far as theories are rationalizations of sentiments, instincts, dispositions of the soul, this is feasible. The chief defect of the novel of ideas is that you must write about people who have ideas to express—which excludes all but ·01 per cent. of the human race. Hence the real, the congenital novelists don't write such books. But then I never pretended to be a congenital novelist.'

I have taken that last sentence as the motto for this chapter because of its importance in removing misunderstandings. Huxley is not congenitally a novelist, and yet, of all his work, his novels—particularly *Point Counter Point* and *Brave New World* (which is nearly a poem)—are likely to last longest.

Primarily, congenitally, Huxley is an essayist, a writer of the form of prose most adapted to reflection and rumination. He is a man who is constantly talking to himself. The audience which a writer, consciously or unconsciously, has in mind while he is composing is one of the most important influences in shaping the style and character of his work.

Huxley never addresses any but the most intelligent, cultured, clear-souled of audiences : himself. Hence the unfailing distinction of his writing. Hence too, in some measure, his ironic humour. Even while he is amusing his audience, he can be amused at it.

The charm of the short essay, as of the diary, is that nothing need be worked out to the bitter end. And when you are addressing so appreciative and responsive an audience as Aldous Huxley, there is a great temptation to let a phrase stand for a paragraph, a paragraph for a page, knowing that the audience is quick enough to understand. The more serious kinds of essay such as are contained in *Proper Studies* and *Do What You Will* are works of self-clarification. Their first use is for the writer; then for such readers as have encountered the same problems. Being primarily practical, they are likely to be superseded.

The most enduring of human faculties is the creative imagination. Aristotle, speaking in the dry, matter-of-fact manner of the medical man, prescribes that to be a poet you must have a command of metaphor. He knows that metaphors are the coagulation of the imagination. They are the hard, bright diamonds of the mind. But metaphors are for poets. What if you are a prose-writer? The metaphors of the prose-writer are his characters. Huxley's Gumbril in *Antic Hay* is his equivalent of Eliot's *The Waste Land*. Sidney Quarles, with his pitiful history, is the prose-writer's way of saying:

> I have heard the mermaids singing, each to each.
> I do not think that they will sing to me.
>
> .   .   .   .   .   .
>
> We have lingered in the chambers of the sea
> By sea-girls wreathed with seaweed red and brown
> Till human voices wake us, and we drown.

Hence it follows that the most metaphorical, the most imaginative and the most enduring of prose forms is the novel. It demands a greater effort than the essay, but is proportionately more rewarding.

To be a congenital novelist is to be, primarily, a story-teller. It means that the naturally most satisfying form of imaginative expression is to answer the question : ' And then . . . and then ? ' Anything else is added by training, deliberately cultivated interests, social demands. To the congenital novelist the story comes easily. Such writers are seldom of the first class.

Most important contemporary writers of fiction appear to be congenitally something else. The reason for their success in fiction is, I think, that they are artists who have not been satisfied to do only what came easily to them, and, faced with the challenge of the difficult novel form, have put forth a more than ordinary imaginative effort. The result has been correspondingly above the ordinary. Much of the attention paid to the novel by writers not naturally novelists is no doubt due to fashion. Twenty-five years ago, men naturally poets, dialecticians, social reformers turned to the theatre as their easiest compromise with the public. To-day, they find it in the novel.

Huxley, naturally an essayist, can discourse elegantly without effort. But the temptation of a wider public, which even the most austere of writers must sometimes feel, and the desire to go beyond what is easy have brought him to the novel. And, for all his detachment, Huxley is passionately interested in the world about him. He has a great naturalist's concern for the human specimens he encounters. (' By nature a natural historian, I am ambitious to add my quota to the sum of particularized beauty-truths about man and his relations with the world about him.'—*Vulgarity in Literature.*)

To preserve his captures, only the novel is adequate. He has to go outside the narrow scope of the essay, his natural form of expression.

Philip Quarles remarks of the novel of ideas that its great defect is that it is a ' made-up affair. Necessarily,' he says, ' for people who can reel off neatly formulated notions aren't quite real ; they're slightly monstrous. Living with monsters becomes slightly tiresome in the long run.'

This is, indeed, the defect of the Peacockian novel of ideas. It is a defect from which Huxley has usually escaped. His Illidge is a Communist, but he is also a man with an inferiority complex, driven by it to murder. His Everard Webley is a Fascist, but also a man in love.

One character only in *Point Counter Point* is slightly monstrous, and that is Rampion. We are shown so little of Rampion's private, personal life, in proportion to the number of times he propounds his doctrine, that now and then he ceases to be a real person, and becomes, let us say, a gramophone record.

It would be possible to argue that, since Rampion is one of the principal melodic themes of *Point Counter Point*, we may expect to find this theme repeated, with variations, again and again. The defect lies, I think, in the fact that the variations are not significant enough. The 'wholeness' theme is not developed with a richness at all comparable to that given to the 'self-division' theme. Numerous characters exemplify 'passion and reason.' Two alone demonstrate 'wholeness.'

In the murder of Everard Webley and in the astonishing scene of Spandrell's suicide to the accompaniment of Beethoven's *heilige Dankgesang*, the whole vast composition of the novel, the wide counter-point of character and event, rises with an urgent, sweeping rhythm to its final climax.

The book has no centre. It is not meant to have one. Huxley does not aim at the spare, symmetrical form. He is no classicist in that sense. At any given moment, almost any of the characters may seem to be the principal, may appear the heart of the book. First it seems to be Walter Bidlake. Then Rampion, then Philip Quarles, then Everard Webley, then, near the end, Elinor Quarles, especially when the double tragedy of her son's death and her potential lover's murder overwhelm her. But it is none of these. It is not even Spandrell, that curiously Dostoieffskian character, though it is in terms of his discovery of Heaven in a world he had thought nothing but dirt and stupidity that the climax of the novel is stated.

If so intentionally various a work has a unity at its heart, that unity is, I think, a question. And a question asked in the full tragic awareness that there can be no answer. That question was stated at the beginning of the book in terms of music. It is so at the end. We remember Pongileoni's snout, the stretched intestines of lambs and the eternal verities. ' Is it illusion or the revelation of the profoundest truth ? ' So again : ' Heaven, in those long-drawn notes, became once more the place of absolute rest, of still and blissful convalescence. . . . And then suddenly there was no more music : only the scratching of the needle on the revolving disc.'

The first hint we have that there is to be a murder comes in Spandrell's lively description of Illidge on page 214 :

' So, to restore his prestige,' says Spandrell, ' he had to change the subject and begin talking about political murder and its advantages with the most wonderfully calm, detached, scientific ferocity. I only laughed at him. " One of these days," I threatened, " I'll take you at your word and invite you to a man-shooting party." And what's more, I will.'

Then again, after Illidge has interrupted at a meeting of Everard Webley's British Freemen and got a black eye, Spandrell taunts Illidge with his lack of courage to attempt the murder of Webley. Illidge, in furious anger, talks recklessly on of what he would do. ' Like a man who stops shouting because he is afraid his voice may break, he was suddenly silent. Spandrell slowly nodded. " All right," he said mysteriously. " All right." '

This comes 250 pages further on. Between the two
there has been no indication of the approaching
murder. On page 506 we are getting nearer. Elinor
Quarles is at home, waiting for Everard to call on
her. Already on page 402 we have been told of the
lonely situation of the Quarles's house.

There comes a knock on the front door. Elinor,
subject to nervous terrors when alone, is frightened
to answer the knock. ' The idea that there was some-
body there, waiting, listening, a stranger, an enemy
perhaps (for Elinor's fancy was pregnant with horrible
hairy faces peering round corners, with menacing
hands, with knives and clubs and pistols) . . .—this
was a nightmare to her, a terror.' The knock is
repeated. She looks out of the window and sees that
it is Spandrell. Opening the door to him she apolo-
gizes for her fears : ' I thought it was at least a
murderer.'

' Spandrell gave vent to brief and noiseless laughter.
" But it might still be a murderer, even though it is
me." '

He has not yet planned the assassination, but the
idea is in the forefront of his thoughts.

After a minute or two's conversation, a telegram
comes, summoning Elinor down to the country where
her child is ill. She asks Spandrell to ring up Webley
at his office, tell him that she will be unable to meet
him that evening, ' Because he was supposed to be
meeting me here at six.'

' " Here ? " ' Spandrell asks, suddenly interested.
' " I won't forget," he assured her emphatically, and

there was still something about his expression which made her suspect a private significance behind the obvious words.'

Elinor leaves a note for her husband, asks Spandrell to give him his keys which he has left behind, and departs.

'Spandrell walked slowly up to Hyde Park Corner. From the public call-box in the station he telephoned to Illidge.'

A quick, vivacious description of Webley leaving his office, jumping into his car and driving to the Quarles's house at the end of the secluded mews follows. He finds the front door open. He calls 'Elinor!' There is no answer. Entering the silent room he catches sight of the message to Philip pinned on a screen. '... a sound behind him made him turn his head. A man was standing within four feet of him, his hands raised; the club which they grasped had already begun to swing sideways and forward from over the right shoulder. Everard threw up his arm, too late. The blow caught him on the left temple. It was as though a light had been suddenly turned out. He was not even conscious of falling.'

A comic interlude with Sidney Quarles ill in bed follows. Then an intensely painful scene with Elinor finding her child moaning with pain. Back again to the house of the murder. Illidge is feeling sick. Spandrell jeers and offers him brandy. A precise, matter-of-fact description of Spandrell washing up the blood, with every sound and movement in the

lonely house minutely noted mingles with Illidge's
sudden memories of his childhood. Then :

   ' Spandrell threw the duster on to a chair and
begin to turn down his shirt cuffs.

   In two hours the muscles of the heart contract
and relax, contract again and relax only eight
thousand times. The earth travels less than an
eighth of a million miles along its orbit. And the
prickly pear has had time to invade only another
hundred acres of Australian territory. Two hours
are as nothing. The time to listen to the Ninth
Symphony and a couple of the posthumous
quartets, to fly from London to Paris, to transfer
a luncheon from the stomach to the small intestines,
to read *Macbeth*, to die of snake bite or earn
one-and-eightpence as a charwoman. No more.
But to Illidge, as he sat waiting, with the dead body
lying there behind the screen, waiting for darkness,
they seemed unending.'

In this passage it is not Spandrell or Illidge reflecting; it is the author exercising the privilege of the
creator of seeing with ' a multiplicity of eyes.'

On pages 265 and 266 Philip Quarles has expounded
this ' new way of looking at things that I want to
experiment with.' The essence of this new way is
multiplicity. ' Multiplicity of eyes and multiplicity
of aspects seen. For instance, one person interprets
events in terms of bishops ; another in terms of the
price of flannel camisoles. . . . And then there's the
biologist, the chemist, the physicist, the historian.

Each sees, professionally, a different aspect of the event, a different layer of reality. What I want to do is to look with all those eyes at once. With religious eyes, scientific eyes, economic eyes, *homme moyen sensuel* eyes. . . .' The result, he says, would be ' Queer. A very queer picture indeed.'

Spandrell points out that they must wait till it is dark before stowing the body in Webley's car, and driving away. They sit down to wait. ' Heart-beat followed heart-beat. Each second the world travelled twenty miles and the prickly pears covered another five rods of Australian ground '—medical eyes, astronomical eyes, economic eyes.

' Behind the screen lay the body . . . from the air, the invisible hosts of saprophytics had already begun their unresisted invasion. They would live among the dead cells, they would grow, and prodigiously multiply and in their growing and procreation all the chemical building of the body would be undone, all the intricacies and complications of its matter would be resolved, till by the time their work was finished a few pounds of carbon, a few quarts of water, some lime, a little phosphorus and sulphur, a pinch of iron and silicon, a handful of mixed salts—all scattered and recombined with the surrounding world—would be all that remained of Everard Webley's ambition to rule and his love for Elinor, of his thoughts about politics and his recollections of childhood, of his fencing and good horsemanship, of that soft, strong voice and that suddenly illuminating smile, of his admiration for Mantegna, his dislike of whiskey, his deliberately terrifying rages, his habit of stroking his chin, his belief in God, his incapacity to whistle a tune correctly, his unshakeable determinations and his knowledge of Russian.'

In this passage the same event, the death of a man, is looked at through biological eyes, chemical eyes, political eyes, *homme moyen sensuel* eyes, aesthetic eyes, religious eyes, a psychologist's eyes and a linguist's eyes.

The reader is not made to weep over a death described in this fashion. He is made to wonder, to doubt. He is shown forcibly the oddity of the universe. It is a manner of dealing with death which is not to be found in any other novelist. No other has had the wide range of erudition to make such a passage natural. It is the deepest heart of Huxley's irony.

Spandrell, looking for God, finds Him and his own death simultaneously. His murder of Webley had merely left him with the knowledge that however hard he tried to escape, he always remained 'living in a kind of dust-heap.' With the murder he had played his last but one card. He would play the last.

The *heilige Dankgesang eines Genesenen an die Gottheit, in der lydischen Tonart* simply had to be heard, he told Rampion.

'It proves all kinds of things—God, the soul, goodness—unescapably.'

He insists that Rampion shall come and hear his gramophone records. Rampion wonders why he is so excited. He does not know that Spandrell is preparing for suicide.

Spandrell reflects : ' The music was a proof ; God existed. But only so long as the violins were playing. When the bows were lifted from the strings, what then ? Garbage and stupidity, the pitiless drought.'

He writes to the British Freemen : ' To-morrow, Wednesday, at five p.m., the murderer of Everard Webley will be at 37 Catskill Street, S.W. 7. . . . He is armed and desperate.'

Even now, the ironic and mischievous devil, of which Huxley is so sharply aware, interrupts. Spandrell, as he reads his note through, is ' reminded of those communications (written in red ink, to imitate blood, and under the influence of the serial stories in *Chums* and the *B.O.P.*), with which he and Pokinghorne Minor had hoped, at nine years old, to startle and terrify Miss Veal, the matron of their preparatory school. . . . "He is armed and desperate." That was pure Pokinghorne.'

The comic name, the ridiculous irrelevance at a moment of great seriousness—that is pure Huxley. It is his characteristic irony, an irony touched now and then with the sardonic, for Huxley has moments of self-hatred. He could not otherwise have created Spandrell.

The next afternoon Rampion arrives to hear the music.

In musical, historical, scientific and religious terms Huxley describes the *heilige Dankgesang*.

'A single violin gave out a long note, then another a sixth above. . . . More than a hundred years before, Beethoven, stone deaf, had heard the imaginary music of stringed instruments expressing his inmost thoughts and feelings. . . . Spiral grooves on a surface of shellac remembered their playing. . . . The archaic Lydian harmonies hung on the air. It was an unimpassioned music, transparent, pure and crystalline, like a tropical sea, an Alpine lake. Water on water, calm sliding over calm; the according of level horizons and waveless expanses, a counterpoint of serenities. And everything clear and bright; no mists, no vague twilights. It was the calm of still and rapturous contemplation, not of drowsiness or sleep. It was the serenity of the convalescent who wakes from fever and finds himself born again into a realm of beauty. But the fever was "the fever called living" and the rebirth was not into this world; the beauty was unearthly, the convalescent serenity was the peace of God. The interweaving of Lydian melodies was heaven.'

Rampion refuses to be convinced. Spandrell feels suddenly tired and depressed. 'Was the proof, after all, no proof? Did the music refer to nothing outside itself and the idiosyncrasies of its inventor?'

The music begins again :

'It was as though heaven had suddenly and impossibly become more heavenly, had passed from achieved perfection into perfection yet more deep and more absolute. The ineffable peace persisted ; but it was no longer the peace of convalescence and passivity. It quivered, it was alive, it seemed to grow and intensify itself, it became an active calm, an almost passionate serenity. The miraculous paradox of eternal life and eternal repose was musically realized.'

Spandrell's doubts vanish. Rampion admits that he is almost convinced, and as we read, we too are reminded of times when music or a fine morning seemed proof of an eternity beyond appearances.

The two passages quoted are perhaps two of the most vivid realizations of the effect of music yet written. To Huxley as he has grown older, music has become increasingly important. In his earlier writings there is little reference to it. Travel, architecture, the plastic arts and literature seem to have been his principal interests. In *Point Counter Point* and in the title essay of *Music at Night* we see how much it means to him now.

Then comes a knocking at the door. Spandrell answers it. There is a deafening explosion, another explosion and another. In the passage three of the British Freemen are looking down at Spandrell's dying body.

'Through the open door came the sound of music. The passion had begun to fade from the celestial melody. Heaven, in those long-drawn notes, became once more the place of absolute rest, of still and blissful convalescence. Long notes, a chord repeated, protracted, bright and pure, hanging, floating, effortlessly soaring on and on. And then suddenly there was no more music ; only the scratching of the needle on the revolving disc.'

Thus Spandrell plays his last card. He has discovered God—or is it only the scratching of a gramophone needle ? Does the world really end ' not with a bang but a whimper ' ? For Spandrell there is no doubt about the bang. Equally for Huxley there is no doubt about either. Both bang and whimper exist. Heaven and the gramophone needle are side by side. ' So seen, reality looks exceedingly queer. Which is how the ironist and perplexed questioner desire it to look.' Huxley will not elect an absolute.

But the novel does not end on a solemn question. Huxley's irony will not allow him to remain in the presence of God, even if only proved by Beethoven. His last gaze, as he surveys the characters that have made up his counterpoint, rests upon Burlap. He seizes upon Burlap in his moment of unctuously accepting the Universe, in his moment of ' whistling " On Wings of Song " with rich expression.' For Burlap has just made the best part of a thousand pounds ; he has successfully capitalized his soulfulness. Further, he has seen the end of Ethel Cobbett, an inconvenient secretary. The fact that she would lie down with her head in a gas oven a few days later was not an event he could foresee. And 'that night he and Beatrice pretended to be two little children and had their bath together. . . . And what a romp they had! . . . Of such is the Kingdom of Heaven.'

So the book ends, with a note of malevolent irony. With the bogus heaven of the religious hypocrite, not with the calm horizons of goodness which was the heaven Spandrell found. Spandrell, for the great part of the book a minor figure, lingers curiously in the memory as having more possibilities of interest than almost any other. Alone among the personages of *Point Counter Point* he is a sinner hungry for goodness. Huxley's only similar figure is the Savage in *Brave New World*. It is a type he rarely invents.

Spandrell is more deeply wounded by self-division than any of the others. With a natural passion for happiness and goodness, a twisted reasoning drives him to unhappiness, and—not to evil—but to ' a piece of squalid knockabout among the dustbins,' to ' garbage and stupidity, the pitiless drought.'

Among the educated of the Western world stupidity has largely taken the place of evil as the opposite of goodness. Very few educated Europeans have a strong sense of evil, of wickedness, of sin. Instead, we are appalled at stupidity. Huxley has a very acute awareness of stupidity. And it enrages him in the same way that evil quite genuinely enrages a Welsh Methodist. Stupidity terrifies Huxley, as it terrifies all intellectuals, because it is something bigger, more primitive than they are, something absolutely uncontrollable and savage. That was why the intellectuals with one voice denounced Hitlerism in Germany. The actual fascist doctrines of the Nazis many intellectuals would have approved. It was the sight of stupidity being given power which infuriated them. Hitler's ' Mein Kampf ' is so *fundamentally* primitive, ignorant and uncultured, that to the intellectual it came as the sin against the Holy Ghost. Followed by the spectacle of all the toughs of Germany doing as they pleased with European culture, it was too much. I doubt if it was simply human charity which inspired the world's intellectuals to protest against the expulsion of Jews, democrats, pacifists, etc. from Germany. Intellectuals are not prone to compassion. It was, surely, much more the fear of the like fate some day ; the fear and the hate which intelligence has of stupidity. The emotion aroused is as intense as that with which goodness fears and hates evil.

So in *Point Counter Point* the opposite to the goodness for which Spandrell thirsts, is not evil, it is stupidity. But his hatred of it is not therefore any the less. And because he has encountered the essential horror of silliness, he seeks and finds his own death.

Let us always remember that a novel is only so many words printed on paper ; in the case of *Point Counter Point* some 180,000 words. The choice of those words and the order in which they are written gives the total combination the nature of an invention, a creation : and a creation of a particular kind, different from every other creation in words. It is a work produced in the same way as a painting, a sculpture, a piece of music, a wall-paper pattern, a chair. Out of the infinity of possible forms, colours, melodic phrases, curves and straight lines the authentic artist selects and arranges a few such elements in a way which is immediately recognizable as having the quality of an invention, of being unique, of being his alone.

The world of Cézanne is not a real world. It is a world of paint. In speaking about it we must never forget the paint. The world of Huxley too is not a real world. We must never forget that it is a world of words. In the past many novelists have been mistakenly praised because of a confusion between words and reality. Scott was once thought a great novelist, because into the reading of his books many readers unconsciously infused feelings connected with romantic holidays in Scotland, admiration for Queen Victoria who cultivated Scotchness, and memories of childhood hours at mother's knee when she read from *Rob Roy*. All these things were part of the real world. The feelings they inspired were perfectly genuine feelings. And similar feelings were for a time inspired by Scott's novels because they referred to the quite genuinely emotive reality. But once readers were no longer preconditioned by that reality, it was found that Scott's novels were, of themselves, unable to arouse the least emotion. The reason was simply that, like many English novelists, he paid too much attention to reality and not enough to words. It is the same with Dickens. He apparently never realized that writing a novel is essentially the same kind of work as carving a figure in granite, or making a dining-table. That some things can be done with the English language and others cannot be done. He has to describe the death of a child, one Little Nell. Good: he plunges into a heavy brooding on the reality of the death of an immature human being; works up a flood of sorrow; is overcome with unhappiness; just as he would be in real life. And for him that is enough. Meanwhile he has completely forgotten that he is dealing in *words*, not reality. He loses all control of them. They just drip out. The result is a misshapen lump, neither useful nor decorative.

Lawrence in the same way frequently forgets the words in his search for reality. It is a mistake Huxley has never made. A long and deliberate cultivation of a natural delight in language has made his respect for his medium instinctive. To throw words about in the way Lawrence does he would have to make a fully conscious effort, an effort which is probably impossible for him.

In writing of *Point Counter Point* I have tried always to remember the words. Those 180,000 words of the novel do indeed call up in the imagination a little world, like the real world, and yet different, and self-subsisting. We can, if we choose, hold that world in the hollow of our hand and speak of its inhabitants as real beings. We can speak of their loves and hates, and the reasons for them, as though they were historical or at least newspaper realities. But to do so will only lead us astray. Those fictional men and women, their loves and hates, are all part of a design planned by one man. *Point Counter Point* is an object the same in kind as a Christopher Wren church, a fount of Caslon type or a Chippendale chair. Its values are simultaneously utilitarian and aesthetic. ' In terms of beauty it enunciates truth.'

' I am ambitious,' says Huxley, ' to add my quota to the sum of particularized beauty-truths about man and his relations with the world about him.' In *Point Counter Point* he has achieved a great part of his ambition.

II

Brave New World

' My own feeling whenever I see a book about the future,' says Huxley in *Do What You Will*, ' is one of boredom and exasperation.'

How then, it may be asked, does Huxley come to be himself writing a book about a topic so disagreeable to him ? The answer is that *Brave New World* is no such book. Not a future civilization, but the present is its subject. And especially all those characteristics of a civilization which is rapidly becoming what may be called a ' wrapped in cellophane ' civilization. By this I mean the valuing of comfort above experience, stability above experiment, so-called science above nature. This temper shows itself in many aspects of daily life. It is in the ridiculous pseudo-scientific jargon of advertising (' Specially made to prevent sore throats!'), in the laziness which prefers tinned to natural food, and films, no matter how bad, to beer and friendly chatter—in the whole clutter of super-fluities which muddle the basis of life in the big cities of Britain and the U.S.A. with artificial needs and artificial supplies, so that the ordinary process of sleeping, eating, drinking and going about one's business has none of the clear vigour and savour it has for less ' efficiency '-ridden peoples.

This is one of the things Huxley is writing about in *Brave New World*. His whole subject is, of course, much bigger than this. The book is a debate on a question which he addresses in the first place to himself, for it concerns that urgent personal problem which we have already seen symbolized in *Point Counter Point* in the persons of Rampion and Philip Quarles—the problem of ' noble savagery ' or in-tellectualism.

This same question is addressed in the second place to a world coming increasingly under the impress of Western, scientific civilization. Is the spread of com-fort, of immunity from disease, from old age—in short, of immunity from life—to be allowed to con-tinue, or should we try to hold back this flood of civilization, as Lawrence thought, and as Huxley is at times inclined to think also.

'I don't want comfort,' says the Savage in *Brave New World*, 'I want God, I want poetry, I want real danger, I want freedom, I want goodness, I want sin.'

Comfort or God. That is the problem debated

in *Brave New World*. A problem of the present, not of the future.

For as the world is going we are getting more and more comfort every day, and yet comfort is proving insufficient for happiness, as the Nazi revolution showed. Much of the impulsive vigour of that revolution sprang from a desire for God, a desire for real danger. The Hitler *Jugend* do not want to be ordinary comfortable men, they want to be heroes.

Poetry, which the Savage also wanted, is valuable in that it is the only way out of otherwise inescapable situations. But as the number of inescapable situations diminishes, so will the need for poetry. Given time, almost everything except death is now escapable. Hence one may either relieve the emotions by thinking that to-morrow will be different, and going to see a psycho-analyst, or by writing a poem. In an age disposed to be scientific, clinical, curative, we prefer time to poetry. We would rather a permanganate-of-potash treatment than a dozen sonnets on the vanities of the flesh.

The need for poetry is going, that for God has largely gone, there is little real danger, little sense of sin, a diminishing amount of freedom, and perhaps too a cooling-off in goodness. Shall we let these things go, do we really prefer comfort? *Brave New World* considers this question from every angle. Brilliantly coloured and lit, the characters symbolizing this problem move before us in a ballet at once farcical and tragic. For if we do want God, and danger, and poetry and sin, are we at the same time prepared to claim the right to be unhappy—'Not to mention the right to grow old and ugly and impotent; the right to have syphilis and cancer; the right to have too little to eat; the right to be lousy; the right to live in constant apprehension of what may happen to-morrow; the right to catch typhoid; the right to be tortured by unspeakable pains of every kind.'

We have to consider whether we are prepared to accept all these things along with the poetry and God.

In *Brave New World* the Savage alone claims them all.

*   *   *

The events described in *Brave New World* take place in A.(fter) F.(ord) 632. That is to say not in a world of the future, but in a world of the imagination, of fantasy. But this fantasy has a logic of its own; it is not a matter of irresponsible meanderings. It is a continuation, a projection, in the strict Euclidean sense, of the real world. When Euclid says ' Produce the line AB to C,' the most surprising things happen to a straight line in the ordinary way unremarkable. Many theorems can only be proved by ' producing ' a line beyond the boundaries of the given figure. In the same way, Huxley in *Brave New World* proves his theorem by continuing the lines of the real world, by ' producing ' those lines, with the result that they extend, not into a ' probable ' future, but into the Looking-Glass. Huxley has taken certain developing growths in present-day civilization, such as, for example, the practice of contraception, and simply

drawn a plan of what those growths will look like
if they develop in the straight line of logical expecta-
tion. 'So seen, reality looks exceedingly queer.' It
is yet another method of securing an ironical effect.

If we examine closely this method of securing an
ironical effect we shall see that it is really a kind of
logical hyperbole, a keying-up of existing colours
to a more intense pitch. For example, Huxley says
in the essay *Obstacle Race* that 'It is obvious that
sexual morality would not have changed as radically
as it has done if the decay of religion had not synchro-
nized with the perfection of a contraceptive technique
which has robbed sexual indulgence of most of its
terrors and, consequently, of much of its sinfulness,'
and goes on to suggest that this is perhaps not entirely
a gain. That same technique has carried off, along
with the terrors, a great deal of passion and vital
interest. Simplified morals seem to produce not
more excitement, but less. In *Brave New World*
Huxley gives parable form to this proposition by
describing a society in which the use of this technique
has been extended, not so much quantitatively as
qualitatively. In A.F. 632 it has become a question
of 'Malthusian drill' and 'hot contraceptives . . .
laid on in every bedroom.' Such intensifications,
such hyperboles raise a laugh in the way that any
exaggeration (a clown's enormous nose, for example)
raises a laugh—by showing us how very like to the
real is the fantastically unreal.

At the same time, just as the clown's full effect
requires an occasional movement of sympathy in

the audience in contrast to its natural attitude of
bellicose hostility—which the clown gets through his
touches of the pathetic—so Huxley mingles his farce
with tragedy. The grotesque popular songs of *Brave
New World* :—

> Hug me till you drug me, honey ;
> Kiss me till I'm in a coma :
> Hug me, honey, snuggly bunny ;
> Love's as good as *soma*.

are an intensification simply of actual popular songs,
are a ' production in the same straight line ' of those
songs. We laugh at the distortion—recognizing the
actual in the imaginary—until we see it through the
eyes of Bernard Marx, to whom these songs are the
expression of everything he is striving against. For
Bernard too wants poetry, sin and goodness. He
longs for passion, not for the ' pneumatic bliss '
offered on every hand in a world where all obstacles
have been taken down. In this world everything is
too easy, it ' does not cost enough.' In short, Huxley
is saying that in present-day Europe and America
everything is either too easy or is rapidly becoming
so. Ought we not to put some of the obstacles
back again, to preserve ourselves from unutterable
boredom ?

Bernard Marx, like Philip Quarles and Hugo
Wenham in *The World of Light*, is Huxley's report
on certain aspects of his own character which he
deplores and would sometimes like to change. Philip
Quarles represents over - intellectualization, Hugo
Wenham the pedantic part of Huxley, and Bernard

Marx, a feeling of inferiority, whether justified or not, in the world of action, of the communal virtues. No one was ever less of 'an admirable committee-man and best mixer' than Huxley. Bernard Marx's feeling of isolation at the Solidarity Service parallels Huxley's own feelings among a crowd of his fellow men. We may note too that Huxley's partial blindness is represented by Philip Quarles's lameness and Bernard's alcohol in his blood-surrogate. 'Too little bone and brawn had isolated Bernard from his fellow men, and the sense of this apartness . . . became in its turn a cause of wider separation.'

Marx, in the novel, plays the part of a John the Baptist to the Jesus Christ of the Savage. The book is the story of these two characters. They symbolize Huxley's reaching out after the values extolled by Lawrence, and thus carry a stage further the debate entered upon in *Point Counter Point*. In *Brave New World* Huxley is convinced of the wisdom of Lawrence's teaching. 'There is a lot in Lawrence that irritates me,' Huxley told me in June 1934, 'but I think he is right.'

*   *   *

Interesting as *Brave New World* is for the ideas it contains, it is perhaps even more fascinating from a technical point of view, and I shall devote some space to this aspect.

Superficially considered, the book is a *conte* of the kind made famous by Voltaire's *Candide*. It is a philosophic essay written in terms of individual

adventure. But whereas Voltaire's method of presenting his story is simple narration, Huxley's method is
dramatic, and even parts of the story which one might
expect to be told in narrative are handled dramatically.

I have already referred to Huxley's sensitive
awareness of his medium, of his sensuous feeling for
words as a material which can be used in certain ways
and not in others. That is a characteristic he has
always shown. In *Brave New World* he manifests
a more than usual concern for surface, for texture.
A novelist who cares for technique is constantly
aware of a difference of texture between passages
consisting of description, those containing psychological or other reflections, and passages of dialogue,
and one of his chief tasks is to join these different
surfaces in such a way that there are no raw edges
and no breaks in the design which must flow on
vigorously from beginning to end. One of the
biggest obstacles to a fine surface is dialogue. It is
more difficult to weave in than anything else. A
surface may be obtained by dodging the difficulty
and dispensing with dialogue, as for instance Pater
does in *Marius the Epicurean*. That achieves a very
fine texture. It is perhaps a little too silky, a little
boring at times—for to be lively and vivid, dialogue
is essential. How to keep the dialogue and yet not
spoil the surface is the problem.

More than anything, the ' he said ' and ' she said '
of dialogue menace the surface. These odd little
bits of wooden scaffolding stick up, make rough
edges everywhere. They are boring to write and

tiresome to read. For proof of this compare the effort of reading aloud a passage of Dickens or Lawrence and a passage of Huxley. Huxley has always cast his dialogue as much as possible in dramatic form, omitting the 'he saids' and 'she saids' which, as he says, he gets so sick of writing. The same objections apply equally to any other stage directions, to all 'they wrote,' 'I indicated' and 'we considered' phrases. For the alert reader these bits of scaffolding are indeed unnecessary. Now, in the opening chapters of *Brave New World*, Huxley goes even further than he has been accustomed to, and by the use of italics and a kind of contrapuntal writing of dialogue is able to indicate who is acting without any stage directions whatever coming between the action and the reader. And at the same time he achieves a surface, hard and gleaming as steel, superbly in keeping with the character of the story.

The book opens with a swift and firm setting of the scene. Twenty lines and the dialogue begins. The Director of the Central London Hatchery and Conditioning Centre is showing a new batch of students over the building. The students, like all those new to the game, are heavily loaded with note-books and pencils. Every word of the Director's is treasured. Everything must go down in the note-books :

' "I shall begin at the beginning," said the D.H.C., and the more zealous students recorded his intention in their note-books : *Begin at the beginning.*'

The Director gives a brief description of the modern fertilizing process and the pencils hurry across the page. . . . ' *Responds by budding.* The pencils were busy.'

The next time we meet the italics they are sufficient of themselves to supply direct to one's mind, without the least delay, the idea : ' wrote the students in their note-books.' In a flash the italicized words evoke the picture of the drove of boys following the Director of Hatcheries and Conditioning about the corridors of the vast building. They give movement to a picture which might otherwise be merely static. And at the same time, the surface is not broken by an ugly, but allegedly essential wooden prop. Much rather does this most interesting technical device add quality to the surface. The italicized sentences such as : *Responds by budding, Major instruments of social stability,* etc., inserted into some twenty pages of dialogue and narrative have the effect of a sudden gleam, as of a metallic thread, in an otherwise plain silk texture, or, to use a musical image, of a short striking rhythmic figure bursting into a smooth melody. It is of course a trick, but then art *is* largely tricks. The artist's capacity is shown by the use he makes of them.

Parallel with this use of italics, Huxley develops a kind of contrapuntal dialogue, rapid, and almost metronome-like in movement. It begins on page 9. The Director and Mr. Foster are continuing their explanation of the Centre. They speak alternately :

' " Eighty-eight cubic metres of card-index," said Mr. Foster with relish as they entered.

" Containing all the relevant information," added the Director.

" Brought up to date every morning."

" And co-ordinated every afternoon." '

and so on for a whole page.

The voices pop in and out; Click-clack, click-clack. Like marionettes, like the figures in a Punch and Judy show—fantastic caricatures imitating the real world. On page 37 the method is developed still further and there are alternations, not merely of a single line of dialogue, but of paragraphs of mingled dialogue and narrative.

The story flashes backwards and forwards between Mustapha Mond, the Controller, describing life in the pre-Fordian era—which is frequently written in direct speech, dramatically, and not as something being described—and ' shots ' of two young women of the Centre going about their toilet.

One might be inclined to allege the influence of film technique were it not that Huxley dislikes the cinema and rarely visits it.[1]

In this part of the story too we have a case of that kind of Huxleyan humour exemplified by the ex-fish

[1] Huxley's opinion of the talkies is sufficiently indicated in the essay ' Silence is Golden ' in *Do What You Will*. He says : ' Oh, those mammy-songs, those love-longings, those loud hilarities ! How was it possible that human emotions intrinsically decent could be so ignobly parodied ? I felt like a man who, having asked for wine, is offered a brimming bowl of hog-wash. And not even fresh hog-wash. Rancid hog-wash, decaying hog-wash. For there was a horrible tang of putrefaction in all that music.'

saying ' I do,' in, as it were, an inverted condition. We noticed earlier that the ' ex-fish ' kind of humour might become in time completely unfunny. In *Brave New World* we see the reverse process at work. Words which are not funny to us have become so by A.F. 632. The words ' mother ' and ' father ' are obscene, are smut to the students, and produce either a blush or a grin.

' " In brief," the Director summed up, " the parents were the father and mother." The smut that was really science fell with a crash into the boys' eye-avoiding silence.'

Huxley then makes use of a kind of metonymy— putting the effect for the cause—with humorous results :

The Director ' returned to Little Reuben . . . in whose room, one evening, by an oversight, his father and mother (crash, crash !) happened to leave the radio on . . . and the next morning, to the astonishment of his crash and crash (the more daring of the boys ventured to grin at one another), Little Reuben woke up repeating word for word a long lecture by that curious old writer, George Bernard Shaw. . . . To Little Reuben's wink and snigger . . .'

This metonymy is one of the devices by which Huxley creates the atmosphere of fantasy.

The same device is used on page 38 with great effect, while at the same time a distinct acceleration of tempo is ingeniously introduced :

   ' " You all remember," said the Controller, in his strong deep voice, " you all remember, I suppose that beautiful and inspired saying of Our Ford's : History is bunk. History," he repeated slowly, " is bunk."
   He waved his hand ; and it was as though, with an invisible feather-whisk, he had brushed away a little dust, and the dust was Harappa, was Ur of the Chaldees ; some spider-webs, and they were Thebes and Babylon and Cnossos and Mycenae. Whisk, whisk—and where was Odysseus, where was Job, where were Jupiter and Gotama and Jesus ? Whisk—and those specks of antique dirt called Athens and Rome, Jerusalem and the Middle Kingdom—all were gone. Whisk—the place where Italy had been was empty. Whisk, the cathedrals ; whisk, King Lear and the Thoughts of Pascal. Whisk, Passion ; whisk, Requiem ; whisk, Symphony ; whisk . . .'

The gradual shortening of the clauses in that passage, the feeling of bitterness behind the curt abrupt phrases, combined with the more rapid movement of the last two or three lines, prepare the way for a brisker movement in the story as a whole. For the next twenty-seven pages the relations of the characters, a wider view of the settings of these characters, and of the philosophy of A.F. 632 are represented in a rapid series of brief ' shots,' none longer than a page, which gradually shorten to a line or so each, until the marionettes seem to appear and disappear with the peculiarly hypnotizing effect of assymetrical machinery in swift motion. The jointed arm. of a treadle, an eccentric, a piston-rod, these are the images suggested by the movement of the dialogue. Without a single word of direct description, the sensation of a world of wheels continually turning, of an endless hum and click of machinery, is powerfully conveyed, almost, it seems, direct to the actual nerves and sensibilities of the reader. It is difficult to realize that the impression is being made entirely by indirect means, so powerful is it. And yet the dialogue contains nothing but fragmentary statements concerning the technics of the brave new world set side by side with expressions of emotion, both contemporary and pre-Fordian.

It is difficult to indicate the movement of the prose without lengthy quotation. The point I am stressing is that everywhere Huxley cuts out that scaffolding which is so inimical to a hard, clear surface. Everywhere he presents as much as possible of his material in a vivid, dramatic form, switching from dialogue to direct description and back to dialogue—his sole aim being speed and vivacity, which of themselves necessarily produce a texture at once hard and bright.

Here is an example :

The Controller, Mustapha Mond, is giving the students a lecture :

'Our Ford—or Our Freud, as, for some in-
scrutable reason, he chose to call himself whenever
he spoke of psychological matters—Our Freud had
been the first to reveal the appalling dangers of
family life. The world was full of fathers—was
therefore full of misery ; full of mothers—therefore of every kind of perversion, from sadism to
chastity ; full of brothers, sisters, uncles, aunts—
full of madness and suicide.

"And yet, among the savages of Samoa, in
certain islands off the coast of New Guinea . . ."

The tropical sunshine lay like warm honey on
the naked bodies of children tumbling promiscuously among the hibiscus blossoms. Home was
in any one of twenty palm-thatched houses. In
the Trobriands conception was the work of
ancestral ghosts ; nobody had ever heard of a
father.

"Extremes," said the Controller, "meet. For
the good reason that they are made to meet." '

In this passage the first paragraph is a summary of
what the Controller says. In the second paragraph,
two lines of direct speech. Then, not a summary
again, but an independent and very vivid presentation
of what the Controller is talking about. It is exactly
as though a film producer, dealing with a character
speaking about the Trobriand islands, were to cut in
suddenly with an actual shot of those islands. Here
Huxley, as though he were a ventriloquist, pushes
aside his dummy—the Controller—and speaks with

his own voice, then, for the last two lines of the passage, once more picks up the dummy.

Or again, on page 46 :

' " Think of water under pressure in a pipe." They thought of it. " I pierce it once," said the Controller. " What a jet ! "

He pierced it twenty times. There were twenty piddling little fountains.

" My baby. My baby . . . ! "

" Mother ! " The madness is infectious.

" My love, my one and only, precious, precious . . ."

Mother, monogamy, romance. High spurts the fountain ; fierce and foamy the wild jet. The urge has but a single outlet. My love, my baby. No wonder those pre-moderns were mad and wicked and miserable. Their world didn't allow them to take things easily, didn't allow them to be sane, virtuous, happy.'

This is a kind of polyphonic writing. The author, instead of restricting himself to a single point of view and narrating everything through that, shifts his ground from sentence to sentence. He actually mimes in dramatic form what is merely something described, spoken *about*, by the Controller.

Then, having for three lines acted the passion of mother and child and lovers, he suddenly drops the dramatic mood and becomes the reflective bystander, gradually fading from that into the image of the Controller, now presented only by report, and not as in the first two lines, in the first person. Such Protean impersonation, such a shifting viewpoint, is, to my mind, something new in fiction. I doubt if it can be exactly paralleled from any other author. And this intersection of planes, this polyphonic interweaving of voices, gives an extraordinary richness to the prose. A richness which is not a matter of verbal craftsmanship, but is rather a richness of the intellect and imagination glowing, as it were, underneath or behind the actual prose. And it is this bright richness which makes *Brave New World*, as I have said, almost a poem.

The third chapter and with it the first ' movement ' of the book ends with an amazing tour-de-force of criss-crossing dialogue and narrative. The spotlight flies at high speed from one character to another, never resting for more than a moment. A face gleams out of the darkness, a voice is heard for a second, then disappears to make way for another and another. Then back to the first again, click : a face ; clack : a voice, back and forth. First we have the Controller, then Lenina Crowne, then Bernard Marx, then the Controller, again Lenina Crowne, the Controller, Lenina Crowne, the Controller . . . Thus :

' Bernard hated them, hated them. But they were two, they were large, they were strong.

" The Nine Years' War began in A.F. 141."

" Not even if it *were* true about the alcohol in his blood-surrogate."

" Phosgene, chloropicrin, ethyl iodoacetate, di-
phenylcyanarsine, trichlormethyl chloroformate,
dichlorethyl sulphide. Not to mention hydro-
cyanic acid."

" Which I simply don't believe," Lenina con-
cluded.

" The noise of fourteen thousand aeroplanes
advancing in open order. But in the Kurfursten-
damm and the Eighth Arrondissement, the explosion
of the anthrax bombs is hardly louder than the
popping of a paper bag."

" Because I *do* want to see a Savage Reserva-
tion."

$CH_3C_6H_2(NO_2)_3 + Hg(CNO)_2 =$ well, what?
An enormous hole in the ground, a pile of masonry,
some bits of flesh and mucus, a foot, with the boot
still on it, flying through the air and landing, flop,
in the middle of the geraniums—the scarlet ones :
such a splendid show that summer ! '

For twelve pages the spotlight flashes in this way
hither and thither over the civilization of After Ford.
The cumulative effect is tremendous. The complicated life of a fantastic and yet curiously familiar
civilization is impressed upon the mind and the senses
in a way which a hundred pages of direct description
could never achieve. And at the same time as this
vivid picture is being invoked, the prose in which it is
done, by its very movement and rhythm, by its swift,
metallic flashes, reinforces almost hypnotically the

impression created, precisely as in poetry the effect of the rhythm is to intensify, to drive deeper the sense of the words.

* * *

The ideological core of the book—the problem of which is the more desirable, passion or pleasure, poetry or ' emotional engineering,' comfort or God— is discussed in Chapter 16.

Bernard Marx and his friend Helmholtz Watson have at last incurred through their unorthodoxy the displeasure of the Resident Controller for Western Europe. They are summoned, with the Savage, into Mustapha Mond's study, and the stage is set for a debate on the values of post-Fordian civilization, as compared with those of Shakespeare's civilization.

Mond explains that Shakespeare is banned in A.F. 632; it is a forbidden book. And even though he, Mond, privately thinks that *Othello* is better than the ' feelies,' he contends that Shakespeare would be no longer understood, and that, further, it is now impossible to write in Shakespeare's manner.

' " . . . you can't make tragedies without social instability," he remarks. " The world's stable now. People are happy; they get what they want, and they never want what they can't get. They're well off; they're safe; they're never ill; they're not afraid of death; they're blissfully ignorant of passion and old age; they're plagued with no mothers or fathers; they've got no wives, or children, or lovers to feel strongly about; they're so conditioned that they practically can't help behaving as they ought to behave. . . .

" You've got to choose between happiness and what people used to call high art. We've sacrificed the high art. We have the feelies and the scent organ instead. . . .

" Actual happiness always looks pretty squalid in comparison with the over-compensations for misery. And, of course, stability isn't nearly so spectacular as instability. And being contented has none of the glamour of a good fight against misfortune, none of the picturesqueness of a struggle with temptation, or a fatal overthrow by passion or doubt. Happiness is never grand." '

Turning from art to science, Mond says :

' " It's curious to read what people in the time of Our Ford used to write about scientific progress. They seem to have imagined that it could be allowed to go on indefinitely, regardless of everything else. . . . Our Ford himself did a good deal to shift the emphasis from truth and beauty to comfort and happiness. . . . And, of course, whenever the masses seized political power, then it was happiness rather than truth or beauty that mattered. Still, in spite of everything, unrestricted scientific research was still permitted. . . . Right up to the time of the Nine Years' War. *That* made them change their tune all right. What's the point of truth or beauty or knowledge when the anthrax bombs are popping all around you ? That was when science first began to be controlled—after the Nine Years' War. People were ready to have even their appetites controlled then. Anything for a quiet life. We've gone on controlling ever since. It hasn't been very good for truth, of course. But it's been very good for happiness. One can't have something for nothing. Happiness has got to be paid for." '

After science, religion.

Mond quotes Cardinal Newman as saying that you can only be independent of God while you have youth and prosperity ; independence will not take you safely to the end.

' " Well," says Mond, " we've now got youth and prosperity right up to the end. What follows ? Evidently, that we can be independent of God. . . .

" God isn't compatible with machinery and scientific medicine and universal happiness." '

The Savage quotes *King Lear*.

' " The gods are just," he says. " Have they not used the pleasant vices of civilization as an instrument to degrade man ? If you allowed yourselves to think of God, you wouldn't allow yourselves to be degraded by pleasant vices. You'd have a reason for bearing things patiently, for doing things with courage . . . for self-denial . . . for chastity . . . for everything noble and fine and heroic."

" Civilization," says Mond, " has absolutely no need of nobility or heroism. These things are symptoms of political inefficiency. . . . Anybody can be virtuous now. You can carry at least half your morality about in a bottle. Christianity without tears—that's what *soma* is."

" But tears are necessary. Don't you remember what Othello said ? ' If after every tempest come such calms, may the winds blow till they have wakened death.' . . . What you need here is something *with* tears for a change. Nothing costs enough here." '

Huxley would himself, I think, agree that the tears are necessary. And it is legitimate to ask whether Huxley's angry brooding over a world without tears is not a reflection of a phase of emotional coldness in himself, a sense of emotional inadequacy, of sterility ? *Brave New World* is by far the most pessimistic of his books. In it, for the first time, he faces those political and social questions which he had before left at a distance, because they did not deeply concern him. He was not interested in politics ; but now he was finding that such an interest was forced upon him. Politics was interested in him. The two rival systems for the restriction of freedom—Fascism and Communism—were growing apace through the world. By 1932, when *Brave New World* was published, the high-wage system of Mr. Ford, which in 1928 and 1929 had seemed to Huxley a barrier to revolution, was plainly demonstrating its insufficiency.

But even at a time when he thought that ' In America, under modern capitalism, the whole Prole-

tariat is prosperous and well organized,' Huxley still
hated modern civilization for all those things which
he satirizes in *Brave New World*.

A passage in *Do What You Will* (published in
1929) shows with startling clearness how much *Brave
New World* is a book of the present, not of the future :

> ' The real trouble with the present social and
> industrial system is not that it makes some people
> very much richer than others, but that it makes life
> fundamentally unlivable for all. Now that not
> only work but also leisure has been completely
> mechanized; now that, with every fresh elaboration
> of the social organization, the individual finds him-
> self yet further degraded from manhood towards
> the mere embodiment of a social function ; now
> that ready-made, creation-saving amusements are
> spreading an even intenser boredom through ever
> wider spheres,—existence has become pointless and
> intolerable.'

It is no answer, in Huxley's view, to say that the
mass of the people do not find these creation-saving
amusements boring, that, on the contrary, they obtain
an Aristotelian catharsis from those talkies which to
Huxley taste of hog-wash. For while he agrees that
the mass has not yet realized this boredom, nevertheless, he maintains, it has an objective existence. At
present it is only appreciated by the intelligent. But
a time will soon come when every one will consciously
realize the ' unlivableness ' of life under the present
system. Then, he thinks, will come a revolution,

not communistic, but utterly nihilistic, a destruction of everything. It is the sort of revolution the Savage tried to start when he threw out of the window the *soma* tablets of the Deltas in *Brave New World.*

But for the majority of people, surely, life has not become pointless and intolerable. Huxley is, I fear, merely endeavouring to make a private feeling bearable and dignified by giving it an objective status. Modern civilization becomes from time to time insupportable, for the reasons that Huxley gives, *only* to the intelligent. And in such moods, the intelligent man is apt to give way to that superfluous altruism which even the most strong-minded cannot always resist, and to worry unnecessarily about the multitude, transferring to it a number of private disgusts of which the multitude is meanwhile cheerfully free.

A little reflection does indeed show, as I have already indicated, that our ' wrapped in cellophane ' civilization is ridiculous and stupid. But these considerations can hardly be of much moment to those whose chief task is to get enough to eat. The intense boredom which the present social and industrial system inflicts on the intelligent is by way of being a luxury emotion. It is a by-product of that leisure which gives the educated and comfortably-off opportunity for culture. Everything, as Huxley himself frequently points out, must be paid for. Boredom is the price you pay for leisure and culture. The individual has to decide whether the values of culture are worth the price.

But even though the Savage failed in his individual

iconoclastic revolution, there is a way out, there is an escape from boredom, and this is the doctrine of 'balanced excess,' of all-inclusiveness, which Huxley expounds in *Do What You Will*. It is, of course, a solution for the gifted individual only.

Even if the spread of education does gradually make this way of life possible to an increasing number of people, nevertheless it will probably be agreed that for some time to come only some form of Socialist or Communist philosophy will seriously attract the masses. Huxley has criticized the Marxian creed, but though he has written on this and other political theories, he is, or at least was, indifferent to the day-by-day preoccupations of politics. But *Brave New World* shows such an acute concern for the problems of social organization, and such a disgust at existing methods, that it would not be surprising if Huxley eventually followed the example of André Gide and André Malraux and decided to support Communism as the best alternative, even if itself imperfect, to the Brave New World that is already coming into being.

III

Those Barren Leaves

In *Those Barren Leaves* are to be found preliminary hints of a number of ideas, attitudes and problems developed further in *Point Counter Point* and *Brave New World*. It is a curious book. In parts more entertaining and more wittily farcical than any other of Huxley's novels, it has also a few sections that are by comparison almost dull. It is easy to read—perhaps too easy—a fact of which Huxley seems to be aware when he makes Francis Chelifer say: 'Style pours out of my fountain-pen. In every drachm of blue-black ink a thousand *mots justes* are implicit, like the future characteristics of a man in a piece of chromosome. I apologize.' It is doubtless because the book is for the most part so entertaining and so easy to read, while at the same time having more substance than its two predecessors, *Crome Yellow* and *Antic Hay*, that it is, so far as I can discover, the most popular of Huxley's novels among reasonably intelligent readers.

In form, *Those Barren Leaves* follows the model, exemplified by Peacock's *Crotchet Castle*, of a number of persons gathered together in a country house and conversing at length on various departments of culture, a form which Huxley had already used in *Crome Yellow*. It is not suggested that there is any deliberate imitation. Like temperaments call for like expression. Peacock was, like Huxley, a man of wide erudition. The *Crotchet Castle* form provides admirable opportunities for the exploitation, in the interests of comedy, of that erudition. So long as Huxley keeps closely to this kind of structure, he is at his best. It is when he wishes to make things happen, when he introduces action, that the *longueurs* approach. The most outstanding example of this is the passage describing Mr. Cardan's meeting with Miss and Mr. Elver in Chapter VI and VII of Part III. There are, too, the scenic descriptions, which, though neatly done, stand back too far from the characters to be interesting. They are, as it were, a cardboard setting, efficiently and indeed elegantly painted, but none the less evidently cardboard. The landscape never becomes a part of the lives of the characters as does the palace of the Cybo Malaspinas which constitutes the spiritual setting for the whole story. In this matter of scenery also Huxley appears to be self-conscious, aware of a possible fault, a little nervous as to whether his descriptions are necessary. Francis Chelifer, the autobiographical hero of much of the story, remarks with sardonic self-depreciation, after several pages of description : ' Few things are more profoundly boring and unprofitable than literary description.' I think we may without injustice assume that this is Huxley self-consciously criticizing himself.

A kind of self-consciousness, of uncertainty is in fact what distinguishes *Those Barren Leaves* from both the preceding and succeeding novels. In *Crome Yellow* and *Antic Hay* Huxley does perfectly what he sets out to do. The only adverse criticism possible in the case of those books is one which really lies outside the rights of criticism—that is to say, it is a moral criticism, a criticism of the value of the author's actual aim, not of his means to that end. Within their limits Huxley's first two novels are masterly pieces of work. We may, if we choose, object that those limits are soon reached. We may, but to do so involves the most far-reaching discussion of ultimate values, personal both to Huxley and the critic. In this essay I am trying to keep within the limits of the subject. It is sufficient merely to indicate the possibility of a wider criticism.

Now, the peculiar interest of *Those Barren Leaves* is that it seems to show an awareness in the author of the limitations of subject in *Crome Yellow* and *Antic Hay* and a desire to go beyond those limitations. Huxley appears now to be anxious to deal with more varied aspects of life than he had previously done. Further, he writes now in a greater variety of mood. The satire, the farcical hyperbole, the love of the odd and fantastic are still there, but these moods are mingled with sympathy, with melancholy, with tenderness. Yet while Huxley appears anxious to get outside the satirical and sardonic, to attain a gentler, warmer attitude towards life, he remains at the same time extremely aware of the dangers of so doing, the dangers of a lapse into sentimentality. He is almost too afraid of making a fool of himself, of giving himself away. And at every moment we are constantly aware of the ironic part of Huxley's self observing him as he writes. At every moment we expect, and frequently get, an ironic incursion into the tenderness, the passion or the sadness which he has momentarily permitted himself. In no novel of Huxley's is the sensation of this duality so sharp as in *Those Barren Leaves*.

The experience of this duality, of the little mocking devil sitting within the mind, ever ready to pounce upon some unguarded moment, is an experience well known to writers. ' This second me,' says Alphonse Daudet, ' I have never been able to intoxicate, to make shed tears, or put to sleep. And how it sees into things, and how it mocks!'[1] Daudet might almost be describing Huxley, so well does this statement fit. Such an awareness of one's second self was uncommon among the major writers of the last century. They appear to have dealt with the problem, if it ever confronted them, as it must be presumed to have done, on any assumption that human nature does not greatly change in a century, by simply repressing the little devil along with all other tabooed phenomena. Most so-called 'great' writers have done the same. Dickens and Victor Hugo are the types of this kind of writer, a kind which is now out of harmony with contemporary feeling and thought. Modern writers tend to take the opposite course—they encourage the little devil. Huxley has done this to a fuller and more profitable extent than most. He has made it the basis of his imaginative work. In his writings the mocking devil and the passionate and weeping human being fight a perpetual duel which is never decided.

Those Barren Leaves begins by giving the little devil full play. Then, in the section entitled *Fragments from the Autobiography of Francis Chelifer*, he is pushed aside and the passional human being speaks, though not without frequent interruptions from the devil. He is given the stage again in *The Loves of the Parallels* and *The Journey*, to be almost, though not quite banished in the final section *Conclusions*, where humanity tempered by philosophy has the last word.

[1] Notes sur la Vie. Quoted by William James : *Varieties of Religious Experience.*

It is this constant see-saw of advantage between the
devil and the human being, worked out in the field of
personal human relationships, which gives *Those
Barren Leaves* its peculiar quality. The see-saw
movement was always present in Huxley's novels. In
Crome Yellow and *Antic Hay* the advantage lies chiefly
with the devil; in *Those Barren Leaves* with the
human being, while in *Point Counter Point* thesis and
antithesis seem to approach, at any rate, a synthesis.

The duality personally experienced by Huxley is
expressed directly in two characters of the story who
are themselves writers—Mary Thriplow, the brilliant
young novelist, and Francis Chelifer, the poet, grimly
determined to love the lowest when he sees it, determined in fact to seek out the lowest. The mocking
devil is responsible too for Mrs. Aldwinkle, one of
the most exhilarating satirical portraits Huxley has
ever done. Now and then Huxley gives a touch of
sympathy to the old woman, and he does so with such
tact that we feel he has portrayed her as she is, without
malice, without caricature. Brilliant though the surface is, we are aware also of the depth below it. The
creation of Mrs. Aldwinkle is a triumph of the fantastic, saved from inexpressive exaggeration, because
that creation remains comic and therefore human.

The portrait of Mary Thriplow is a portrait of
modern self-consciousness. She is the modern,
sophisticated intelligence which regards itself with
distrust and the emotions with an extravagant respect.
Perhaps even in 1924 Huxley was beginning to suspect
that the cautious intellectualism which education and

circumstances had caused him to cultivate so intensely
was inadequate. Huxley did not see a great deal of
Lawrence till 1926 onwards ; but it looks as though
he were ready for a good deal of Lawrence's teaching
before he met him. In *Those Barren Leaves* he is
still suspicious of the emotions, all the more so because his mocking devil notes with so keen a relish
the ridiculousness of deliberately cultivated emotion.

Note in the following passage how ingeniously the
little devil gets in his mocking laughter by the use
merely of punctuation and the turn of phrase.

Miss Thriplow is anxious to appear to Calamy
simple and unsophisticated, to be the possessor of a
child-like heart :

> ' " I think it's difficult to be genuine," Miss
> Thriplow went on, " if one's a celebrity or a public
> figure, or anything of that sort." She became very
> confidential indeed. " I get quite frightened when
> I see my name in the papers and photographers
> want to take pictures of me and people ask me out
> to dinner. I'm afraid of losing my obscurity.
> Genuineness only thrives in the dark. *Like celery.*"
> *How little and obscure she was ! How poor and*
> *honest, so to speak.*'

The italicized words are the mocking devil's part.
Like celery. Miss Thriplow's carefully cultivated
mind, apt at finding the ingenious image, here bursts
through the mask of simplicity which she is trying so
hard to wear. That *Like celery* gives her away. The
devil speaks through her mouth, though he might

well have spoken through the mouth of a bystander. *Like celery.* It is the retort of a sarcastic observer to the self-consciousness of *Genuineness only thrives in the dark.* That retort is made all the more diabolical by being put into the victim's mouth, without her realizing in the least its implications.

In the next sentence, *How little and obscure she was !* the devil is speaking through the bystander, in this case the author. In that sentence Huxley is giving the thought of his character together with the sarcastic comment of his own little devil. If he were observing Mary Thriplow softly and tenderly as Tchehov might have done, he would have written something like this : ' And it seemed to her then that she was a little woman, of no importance.' But Huxley cannot treat Mary Thriplow gently, because he is so anxious to avoid such a failing in himself. Instead he mocks. The interjectory shape of the phrase, the exclamation mark, are the voice of mockery. The words are said with a sardonic smile, because the author resents such weaknesses in human nature. He has perhaps caught himself falling into just such a weakness.

Again, a few pages further on : ' Why she had ever thought of pretending she was anything but simple and natural she couldn't now imagine. After all, that was what she really was—or at least what she had determined that she ought to be.'

That last clause, ' or at least what she had determined that she ought to be,' is the devil's mocking comment on Mary Thriplow's self-deception.

On page 53 we have Miss Thriplow's complaint about her books not being understood :

' " They always seem entirely to misunderstand what one writes," Miss Thriplow went on. " They like my books because they're smart and unexpected and rather paradoxical and cynical and elegantly brutal. They don't see how serious it all is. They don't see the tragedy and the tenderness underneath. You see," she explained, "I'm trying to do something new—a chemical compound of all the categories. Lightness and tragedy and loveliness and wit and fantasy and realism and irony and sentiment all combined. People seem to find it merely amusing, that's all." '

Compare this description of Mary Thriplow's novels with the characteristic qualities of *Those Barren Leaves*, or, indeed, of any of Huxley's fiction. It is a surprisingly close description of that fiction. I suggest that in this passage Huxley is laughing a little sardonically at complaints he had himself sometimes uttered of not being understood. Huxley knows very well what it is to feel failure, to feel a pessimism which can only be relieved by sardonic expression. And though he may laugh lightly at his own complaints, as he does in the passage just quoted, he feels, and I think justly, that those complaints are not exaggerated.

Mr. Cardan comments on Miss Thriplow's remarks : ' " You write sentimental tragedies in terms of satire and they see only the satire. Isn't it to be expected ? " '

Mr. Cardan's comment is to be expected. Huxley

is able to see himself sufficiently objectively to be able
to give the rational, common-sense point of view.
He sees it but cannot agree with it.

It might be objected that one is not justified in
making these deductions from matter that is presented
in a purely dramatic form in a novel. But I think it
will be agreed, as I have said earlier, that an author
cannot help putting himself into every character he
creates. He may do it consciously or he may do it
unconsciously. Probably more often the latter.
But some part of him is there, none the less. And
when you are dealing with the complicated, self-
conscious states of mind which express themselves
in the sardonic, in irony and sarcasm, it is difficult even
for the writer to say what he ' really ' means. He
does not know what he ' really ' means, because that
sought-for reality is not a constant thing. As Huxley
has himself often pointed out, the individual is never
one consistent person, but a congeries of diverse
states of being. It may seem to a writer at any given
moment that what he wrote at some previous moment
is quite contrary to what he ' really ' is. But this is
a purely arbitrary decision. We may find an analogy
by considering the case-forms of a noun in an inflected
language, such as German. Which is the ' real ' word?
The Nominative form, the Accusative, the Dative
Plural ? None of them. The real word is the whole
series of forms. What a writer really means is everything he has written. His impersonations are himself,
actual or potential. And the substance of Mary
Thriplow's remarks lies too close to Huxley's own

art for it to be possible to contend that those remarks are intended merely as dramatically appropriate and in character.

In Mary Thriplow, the brilliant young novelist with her notebooks in which she so earnestly records her ' nice feelings,' her epigrams and those of other people, Huxley has created with a subtle malice the perfect type of modern, self-conscious professional writer. It is partly a self-criticism—just as Philip Quarles in *Point Counter Point* is a more patient self-criticism—and partly a criticism of every professional writer. Has there ever been one who did not keep, like Mary Thriplow, a diary ' merely for the sake of keeping her emotions in training ' ?

' Wasn't she deliberately scratching her heart to make it bleed,' thinks Miss Thriplow, ' and then writing stories with the red fluid ? '

This is Huxley's comment on the whole professional literary business.

But interesting though the psychological line of enquiry is, it must not exclude the aesthetic. *Those Barren Leaves* presents several features which, if not unique in Huxley's fiction, are at least most strongly developed in this novel.

In his lecture on his grandfather, *T. H. Huxley as a Man of Letters*, Huxley says :

' From the neat antithesis to the odd and laughter-provoking word—Huxley used every device for the expression of sarcasm and irony.'

In that sentence Aldous Huxley might well have

been noting a characteristic of his own work. 'The
odd and laughter-provoking word' is the whole basis
of one famous humorous passage in *Crome Yellow*.
Extended into a phrase it is the inspiration of the short
story, *Eupompus Gave Splendour to Art by Numbers*.
In *Those Barren Leaves* the odd word and the fantastic
piece of information provide several passages of
delightful intellectual fooling. One, written with
tremendous bravura should be quoted :

'Dinner was served in the Saloon of the Ancestors. In Mrs. Aldwinkle's enthusiastic imagination
what marvellous symposia had been held within
those walls—centuries even before they were built
—what intellectual feasts! Aquinas, here, had
confided to an early Malaspina his secret doubt on
the predicability of rollations, had twitted the robber
marquess, over a goblet of wine, with the feebleness
of his synderesis. Dante had insisted on the
advantages of having a Platonic mistress whom
one never met and who could, when necessary, be
identified with Theology. Peter of Picardy, meanwhile, on his way to Rome had recited from his
rhymed version of *Physiologus* the lines on the
Hyaena, a beast which, besides being an herma-
phrodite, carries in its eye a stone which, held by a
man in his mouth, permits him to see the future ;
it symbolizes moreover avarice and lasciviousness.
Learned Boccaccio had discoursed on the genealogy
of the gods. Pico della Mirandola, over the boar's
head, quoted the kabbala in support of the doctrine

of the Trinity. Michelangelo had expounded his
plans for the façade of San Lorenzo in Florence.
Galileo had speculated why it is only up to thirty-
two feet that Nature abhors a vacuum. Marini
had astonished with his conceits. Luca Giordano,
for a wager, had painted, between the roast and the
dessert, a full-sized picture of Hannibal crossing
the Alps. . . . And then, what brilliant ladies
heightened the lustre of these feasts! Lovely,
perennially young, accomplished as the protagon-
ists of Castiglione's *Courtier*, amorous in the
extreme—they inspired the men of genius to yet
higher flights, they capped their hardiest sallies
with a word of feminine grace.

It had been Mrs. Aldwinkle's ambition, ever
since she bought the palace, to revive these ancient
glories. She saw herself, unofficially a princess,
surrounded by a court of poets, philosophers and
artists. Beautiful women should swim through
the great saloons and the gardens, glowing with
love for the men of genius. And periodically—
for the apartment of the dwarfs, which the Cybo
Malaspina, in imitation of the Gonzaga, had in-
cluded in their palace, demanded appropriate
inhabitants to furnish it—periodically they should
bring forth, painlessly, children to the men of
genius—all curly-headed, fully toothed and two
years old on the day of birth, and all infant prodi-
gies. Rows of little Mozarts. In a word, the
palace of Vezza should re-become what it had
never been except in Mrs. Aldwinkle's fancy.'

This is a magnificent piece of that kind of baroque writing which, as Huxley says, is particularly suited to comedy : ' Styles that protest too much are not fit for serious, tragical use. They are by nature suited to comedy, whose essence is exaggeration.' The passage quoted above is an admirable example of the truth of this remark.

The style of *Those Barren Leaves* is noticeably more polysyllabic than that of the other novels. Polysyllabism is itself a form of exaggeration, and this is, in all probability, one of the causes of the feeling of light mockery which seems to lurk continually behind even the most serious passages of the book.

In structure the novel is loose and digressive. From page 91 when Francis Chelifer concludes his description of his first view of Mrs. Aldwinkle to page 162 when he meets her again is one long digression. The mood of this digression— one for the most part of a kind of bitterness grown dull through long acquaintance—is so different from the bright and piercing irony of the section entitled *An Evening at Mrs. Aldwinkle's* that it might almost belong to a different book. It is as though the author had written the beginnings of two separate stories and had then made up his mind to combine them. This is done, indeed, most ingeniously. For when Mrs. Aldwinkle reappears after an interval of some seventy pages, she occasions no surprise. We feel we had been expecting her to turn up all the time. Because of its digressiveness and dis-

cursiveness the book has the quality of an impromptu.
We get the impression that the author is inventing as
he goes along. And he invents with such a prodigal
fertility of ideas that we do not have time to question
where all this invention is leading. That this apparently unguided spontaneity is in the end bent and
woven into a pattern is due to Huxley's masterly
feeling for line, for form, which we have already com-
mented on in reference to *Point Counter Point*. Without this final achievement of a pattern the book would
not make half the effect it does. That has been the
weakness of imitators of Huxley, and even of other
genuinely original novelists of a similar kind, such as
Peacock. Their wit, culture and sparkling dialogue
are manipulated to no definite purpose ; they spin
brilliant threads which hang suspended in the air,
materials for a novel rather than the completed work.

All through *Those Barren Leaves* the characters
are in the habit of declaiming little essays on topics
that have interested Huxley. We may even find
them repeating what Huxley has said in his own
essays. Mr. Cardan's remarks on baroque art for
instance are to be found also in *Along the Road.*
But these discursive dialogues and monologues,
although actually personal to Huxley, are spoken
in an accent so well in character and with such
appropriate gestures that we do not feel them to
be intrusive.

I mentioned earlier that *Those Barren Leaves* contained anticipations of *Point Counter Point* and *Brave
New World.* An example is the reflections of Calamy,

who may be taken to represent the voice of philosophy. Speaking of his hand, he says :

> ' " This shape which interrupts the light—it is enough to think of it for five minutes to perceive that it exists simultaneously in a dozen parallel worlds.   It exists as electrical charges ; as chemical molecules ; as living cells ; as part of a moral being, the instrument of good and evil ; in the physical world and in the mind." '

We have here the ' multiplicity of eyes ' way of looking at the universe on which Philip Quarles broods with such fascination and which Huxley himself puts to such good use in *Point Counter Point*.

Calamy is indeed an earlier stage of Philip Quarles, just as Francis Chelifer is of Spandrell.

For instance :

> ' " It's a pity," put in Chelifer, in his dry, clear, accurate voice, " it's a pity that the human mind didn't do its job of invention a little better while it was about it.   We might, for example, have made our symbolic abstraction of reality in such a way that it would be unnecessary for a creative and possibly immortal soul to be troubled with the haemorrhoids."
>
> Calamy laughed.   " Incorrigible sentimentalist ! "
>
> " Sentimentalist ? " echoed Chelifer, on a note of surprise.
>
> " A sentimentalist inside out," said Calamy, nodding affirmatively.'

Chelifer's attitude and the criticism of it are not far from the attitude of Spandrell and Rampion's criticism of him. Chelifer, like Spandrell, is a self-absorbed character.

Close too to the attitude of Bernard Marx in *Brave New World* when he has achieved his ambition of sleeping with the 'awfully pneumatic' Lenina Crowne is that of Chelifer in his love affair. Compare Chelifer saying :

> ' " I was happy, being with Barbara ; I was utterly miserable because I was not with her, so to speak, in the right way ; " with Bernard Marx : " I didn't want it to end with our going to bed." '

Biographical deductions might be made from this attitude which is analysed at some length both in *Those Barren Leaves* and *Brave New World*, and, in its reverse form, in Walter Bidlake. It is the long-meditated problem of ' Passion and reason, self-division's cause.'

We may note too in *Those Barren Leaves* a faint foreshadowing of Helmholtz Watson's problem of writing when there is nothing to write about :

> ' A happy people, we now say, has no history ; and we might add that happy individuals have no literature. The novelist dismisses in a paragraph his hero's twenty years of happiness ; over a week of misery and spiritual debate he will linger through twenty chapters. When there is no more misery, he will have nothing to write about. Perhaps it will be for the best.'

High art or happiness. You cannot have both. The life by values, which is the novelist's chief concern, forces him to concentrate on the week of misery. When there is no longer any misery, life will presumably no longer have value. Which is, in fact, the conclusion reached in *Brave New World*.

IV

Crome Yellow and *Antic Hay*

Crome Yellow, Huxley's first novel, was published in 1921 when he was twenty-seven. By 1921 Huxley had published three books of poetry and one of short stories—*Limbo*, which contained two war stories and other work, nearly all of which was remarkable for a kind of contemptuous anger expressed in ferocious farce. The chief literary influences discernible both in the poetry and the prose were Laforgue, Rimbaud and Anatole France.

Then in *Crome Yellow* Huxley showed himself completely master of his assimilations, a mature novelist. The book is worth examining closely for its technique, its ideas and its acuteness of psychological description. It is a light book, a gay one, and, in comparison with its successors, small in scope. But although easy to read, we shall be mistaken in taking it too easily. To get some preliminary idea of its brilliance, think for a moment of the average capable writer's first novel. What sort of a book does a young man of twenty-seven usually produce? The usual production is described devastatingly in *Crome Yellow* itself:

' " Of course," Mr. Scogan groaned. " I'll describe the plot for you. Little Percy, the hero, was never good at games, but he was always clever. He passes through the usual public school and the usual university and comes to London where he lives among the artists. He is bowed down with melancholy thought; he carries the whole weight of the universe upon his shoulders. He writes a novel of dazzling brilliance; he dabbles delicately in Amour and disappears, at the end of the book, into the luminous Future."

Denis blushed scarlet. Mr. Scogan had described the plan of his novel with an accuracy that was appalling.'

The fact that Huxley is able to see his contemporaries, and also, no doubt, his own immediate past, with such objective clearness is some indication of the natural superiority of his intelligence.

What saves Huxley from the usual self-absorption of the young novelist is his tremendous interest in human beings, most of whom strike him as unfathomably odd and fantastic:

' Denis peeped at them discreetly from the window of the morning-room. His eyes were suddenly become innocent, childlike, unprejudiced. They seemed, these people, inconceivably fantastic. And yet they really existed, they functioned by themselves, they were conscious, they had

minds. Moreover, he was like them. Could one
believe it ? '

Huxley is as fascinated by human beings as a
zoologist at the sight of his first okapi or duck-billed
platypus.

The characters in *Crome Yellow* are the complicated,
civilized, even over-civilized individuals who recur
in all Huxley's novels. There is, first of all, the
author-hero, Denis. He is recognizably of the same
family as Gumbril in *Antic Hay*, Chelifer, Walter
Bidlake, Philip Quarles and Bernard Marx. He is
the intellectual ineffective in action ; a Hamlet type.
Denis's attempts at action, and his weakness for
looking at himself dramatically, from the outside—a
human failing Huxley has often satirically explored—
are admirably introduced in two brief paragraphs :

> ' " A bicycle, a bicycle ! " he said breathless to the
> guard. He felt himself a man of action. . . .
> " All in good time, sir," said the guard sooth-
> ingly. He was a large, stately man with a naval
> beard. One pictured him at home drinking tea,
> surrounded by a numerous family. It was in that
> tone that he must have spoken to his children when
> they were tiresome. " All in good time, sir."
> Denis's man of action collapsed, punctured.'

Or again, Denis thinks of his poem describing the
object of his idealistic love : ' " The Woman who was
a Tree " was what he had called the poem. He had
given her the book when it came out, hoping that the

poem would tell her what he hadn't dared to say. She had never referred to it.'

These tragedies of youth Huxley seems to have experienced as much as any one else, but he is very soon able to regard them with a cool and amused detachment. Sometimes, it is true, his detachment weakens and he appears to take a certain sardonic pleasure in raking over the wound. For the most part, however, he obtains his satirical effects by observing his characters from all angles—within and without— and then describing them with the alarming calmness of a doctor announcing in the quietest tones the imminence of one's death.

Denis, like Huxley, has a voluptuous feeling for landscape and architecture, a sense of the magic of words, and finds also that education makes spontaneous living difficult. But Huxley does not laboriously and humourlessly expound all these peculiarities through page after page of so-called psychological analysis. He presents Denis to the reader gradually. After only nine pages, briefly and vividly presenting Denis, in which we learn that he is twenty-three, in love with Anne (who has not yet appeared), a poet and a good French scholar, a new character, Mrs. Priscilla Wimbush is introduced. She is a high-spirited old lady equally interested in ribaldry, astrology and horse-racing. Following her, five other characters are quickly brought on the scene. In one of them, Mr. Scogan, we recognize the genial, cynical sceptical old gentleman who appears as Mr. Cardan in *Those Barren Leaves*. In Mary Bracegirdle is satirized the blue-stocking of the Freudian epoch, and in Anne we have ' one of the normal types of healthy young womanhood,' the Barbara of *Those Barren Leaves*. Gombauld, the painter, is the type of successful and masterful lover portrayed also in John Bidlake of *Point Counter Point*, the Syrian poet of *Those Barren Leaves*, Helmholtz Watson of *Brave New World*, and Coleman of *Antic Hay*. He is the natural antagonist of the Denis-Walter Bidlake-Gumbril type.

Denis suffers from too much education. ' In the world of ideas,' he says, ' everything was clear ; in life all was obscure, embroiled. Was it surprising that one was miserable, horribly unhappy ? ' And again : ' But, then,' he says to Anne, ' you were born a pagan ; I am trying laboriously to make myself one.' Here, in its earliest stage is the problem which forms the basis of *Point Counter Point*.

More than anything, Denis desires to make Anne love him. The book shows how Denis, as a result of his character, his incapacity for action, fails to achieve his ambition. Denis did not dance, so Anne dances with Gombauld. Denis has not Ivor's easy gallantries, so Anne goes out with Ivor. Denis looks on, rankling with envy. Gombauld is painting Anne's portrait, so Denis has a further cause for jealousy. But from the very intensity of his feeling, choked up behind his shyness and his unfamiliarity with the world, he cannot do more than make Anne pity him. Finally, in despair, he is persuaded by Mary that he must take action, must go away. He sends himself a telegram recalling him to London in haste. ' " One is only happy in action," Denis enunciated, thinking of the telegram.' But no sooner has he taken the decisive step than he begins to regret it. As his last minute at Crome approaches he becomes more and more wretched. The final blow comes when Anne says : ' " I'm wretched you should be going."

' Denis turned towards her ; she really did look wretched. He abandoned himself hopelessly, fatalistically to his destiny. This was what came of action, of doing something decisive. If only he'd just let things drift ! If only . . .'

He is a miniature Hamlet, a type not uncommon among the English.

The construction of *Crome Yellow* is of considerable interest. The story of Denis and Anne, played out against a country-house background, is advanced by the most simple events—a meeting after breakfast, a fall in the dark, dancing to a pianola, a sitting for a portrait—the everyday incidents of a country household in the summer.

Diversifying this story, which we may call the main tune, are a variety of events of different kinds which at intervals interrupt the principal theme. The book is, as it were, a composition in rondo form. That is, if A represents the main tune, and the other letters of the alphabet the other themes, the construction is of the kind : A, B, A, C, A, D, etc.

The B, C, D tunes are represented by the speculative discourses of Mr. Scogan on a wide selection of topics, by the arrival and departure at Crome of other

visitors, Mr. Barbecue-Smith and Ivor Lombard,
by Mr. Bodiham, the parson, and the supremely
comic sermon on ' knops,' by the two self-contained
stories related by Mr. Wimbush about his ancestors,
and finally, by Crome Fair.

One of Mr. Scogan's speculations hints at *Brave
New World* :

> ' An impersonal generation will take the place
> of Nature's hideous system. In vast state in-
> cubators, rows upon rows of gravid bottles will
> supply the world with the population it requires.
> The family system will disappear ; society sapped
> at its very base will have to find new foundations;
> and `Eros, beautifully and irresponsibly free, will
> flit like a gay butterfly from flower to flower
> through a sunlit world.'

This passage was actually suggested to Huxley by
an essay of Leigh Hunt's.

The organization of *Brave New World* is further
discussed by Mr. Scogan in Chapter 22 :

> ' In the Rational State human beings will be
> separated out into distinct species . . . according
> to the qualities of their mind and temperament.
> Examining psychologists trained to what would
> now seem an almost superhuman clairvoyance,
> will test each child that is born and assign it to
> its proper species. Duly labelled and docketed,
> the child will be given the education suitable to
> members of its species, and will be set, in adult

life, to perform these functions which human beings of his variety are capable of performing.'

And so on for several pages.

Brave New World was not published till eleven years after this disquisition was written. The idea of the book was evidently in Huxley's mind all these years. The gleaming brilliance, the vigour and movement of *Brave New World* could not have been achieved without this long, slow brooding of the mind.

Huxley's other novels have more matter in them, a wider range, a greater complexity of pattern, but none has excelled his first in grace, in Mozartian lightness of touch. Real and yet somehow unreal, somehow a fairy-story, a bucolic idyll, *Crome Yellow* haunts the memory like a sunlit wall of peaches seen in childhood, rich with the nostalgic memories of bygone summers. Like the opulent colour of its title, *Crome Yellow* is all of cream and gold.

* * *

In *Antic Hay*, published two years after *Crome Yellow*, we find a vast difference of scope and manner. The ferocious farce of the early short stories is back again, on a larger scale, and even more intense. The cream and gold are gone. We are plunged into the acrid gloom of London in the years immediately following the war.

Of certain sides of life in London during those years it gives an unsurpassed picture. The feeling of the pointlessness of everything, the intentionally senseless diversions, ridiculous games like 'Beaver,' the headlong rush to jazz and drink—anything to forget the war—the whole uneasy movement of the time symbolized so perfectly in the 'Last Ride' (in a taxi) of Mrs. Viveash and Gumbril—all this is captured and described in terms of beauty, pity and humour.

The humour of *Antic Hay* is rough and angry. A bitter and sardonic disgust is forcibly expressed. Huxley, in the character of Gumbril, glimpses in the distance the beauty, truth and goodness which he desires. But what seems to be the very nature of existence makes him despair of reaching that truth, beauty and goodness, because, whenever he gets near, some unforeseen happening whisks him away. These events arise, of course, from the character of Gumbril, who, like Denis, is weak in action. The bitterness resulting from this frustration shows itself in the deliberately extreme silliness of some of the humour, in such witticisms as : ' Where the hormones, there moan I,' or ' There was a young man of East Anglia, whose loins were a tangle of ganglia.' Similar in origin too is the whole elaborate farce of Gumbril's Patent Pneumatic Small-clothes.

Gumbril is a young man too intelligent to be able to put up with the dreariness of a schoolmaster's existence, but insufficiently qualified to do anything else. With the sudden decisiveness of the naturally indecisive, he determines to become rich by commercially exploiting his idea for pneumatic trousers, which, by way of incidental irony, comes to him while attending service in the school chapel. Only by the aid of a beard and a padded overcoat is Gumbril able to summon up sufficient decision to put his intention into practice. But having become rich, his natural weakness reasserts itself and he misses his only chance of happiness through that failing.

Mrs. Viveash, a woman of the Lucy Tantamount species, persuades Gumbril to lunch with her, when he should be going to the country to meet Emily. Gumbril goes with Mrs. Viveash, but he wishes feebly that he had not done so :

> ' He thought of Emily in her native quiet among the flowers. . . . A little absurd, perhaps . . . but exquisite, but adorable, but pure of heart, and flawless in her bright pellucid integrity, complete as a crystal in its faceted perfection. She would be waiting for him ; they would walk through the twiddly lanes—or perhaps there would be a governess-cart for hire, with a fat pony like a tub on legs to pull it. . . .'

Though secretly heavy at heart,

> ' Through the whole meal he clowned away in the most inimitable style. The ghost of a governess-cart rolled along the twiddly lanes of Robertsbridge. But one can refuse to accept responsibility ; a clown cannot be held accountable. And besides, when the future and the past are abolished, when it is only the present instant, whether enchanted or unenchanted, that counts, when there are no causes or motives, no future consequences to be considered, how

can there be responsibility, even for those who
are not clowns ? '

'The ghost of a governess-cart . . .'

That ghost reappears to Gumbril again after the
disaster of Emily's departure from his life. It is his
symbol of goodness and truth—that goodness and
truth which seemed unattainable in the first post-war
years. At that time, many intelligent and sensitive
people, like Gumbril, took refuge in irresponsibility
from the despair which the war had engendered.
Or if not in irresponsibility, in a perpetual quest after
distraction such as that of Mrs. Viveash, or in the
most fantastic blasphemy, like Coleman. *Antic Hay*
is a struggle between despair and hope, in which
despair wins. Despair has the last word in Mrs.
Viveash's : 'To-morrow will be as awful as to-day.'
The sentiment of hope is dispersed in a few precious,
but fugitive moments. It comes in Gumbril's reflection on his one night of love : 'Emily's breasts
were firm and pointed and she slept at last without a
tremor. In the starlight, good, true and beautiful became one.' But despair returns in the next sentence:
'Write the discovery in books—in books *quos*,
in the morning, *legimus cacantes*.'

Antic Hay represents an advance on *Crome Yellow*
in that the characters of it do not remain static as they
do in the earlier book. They develop, they change
under the influence of the events that happen to them.
Gumbril, Shearwater, Rosie, his wife, Lypiatt—these,

at least, pass through decisive changes in their character.

Several of the characters of *Antic Hay* symbolize problems which are further treated in *Point Counter Point*. As a 'natural historian of humanity' Huxley has been fascinated by the peculiarities of certain types, and he studies them again and again, in each of his novels casting a light on a different aspect of the specimens he has chosen. He has studied the problem of the intellectual who has neglected the emotional and physical side of existence—which usually means neglected his wife, *e.g.* Philip Quarles, and in *Antic Hay* the physiologist Shearwater; the problem of the man looking for truth and beauty and goodness but finding only garbage and dust-bins—Spandrell, Chelifer, Gumbril; the problem of the woman who is frightened of physical love—Marjorie Carling and Emily in *Antic Hay*; the type of self-absorbed woman who perpetually and ludicrously sees herself as something larger than life and much more romantic—Mrs. Aldwinkle and Rosie Shearwater; 'the weak, silent man' and the calculating siren—Gumbril and Mrs. Viveash, Walter Bidlake and Lucy Tantamount. One could catalogue and cross-catalogue indefinitely, for though there are parallels, no two characters are ever the same. Certain moral problems recur, because they are problems which Huxley has found to be of inexhaustible interest, but these problems never recur in exactly the same way. They divide and combine and re-combine in a great variety of ways. Put algebraically, if A

plus B minus C equals X in one book, in another
we shall get A minus B plus D equals X, and so on,
through many modifications. For example, only
Spandrell and the Savage are prepared to kill themselves because of their inner disharmony, because of
their failure to attain goodness, but the same problem
concerns, though less urgently, both Gumbril and
Chelifer.

Genius quickly gets taken for granted, and it is,
I think, not sufficiently realized how unusual, how
very remarkable it is that a man of such a capacity
for abstract thought as Huxley should have so deep
an interest in human beings. An interest, moreover,
which is not at all of an abstract kind. I have never
been able to understand that depressingly familiar
comment of both private and professional readers of
Huxley that he despises or dislikes or has a contempt
for humanity. One does not as a rule spend so much
time over one's dislikes. What Huxley's detractors
really mean, I think, is that he has a contempt for
human weaknesses. He has never looked upon mankind's failings with the watery and slightly myopic
eye so dear to the English. If only men and women
would be human! he has said again and again. What
if they are sometimes charitable and generous—animals
are the same, while animals are never so mean and
cruel as human beings are. If only mankind had a
little of the wisdom *homo sapiens* by his name lays
claim to!

The war made human deficiencies more than
usually evident, and they remained so in the post-

war years. *Antic Hay* has preserved that jazz age in crystal. Doubtless it was because it was so truthful a picture of the time—'warts and all'—that it aroused so much shocked indignation. The ordinary human being has a strong psychological resistance to hearing the truth about himself. He cannot bear to look upon his own nakedness.

V

Conclusion

Huxley's novels have not come easily to him. In the twenty years of his writing career he has produced only five, as against nine volumes in the essay form. In each of those five the story is of secondary importance. They would be evidence, without his own admission in Philip Quarles's note-book, that he was not a congenital novelist. The absence of a story no one will regret, since he is able to get on without one. The only justification of the story, really, is that it may maintain the *writer's* interest, may encourage him to go on to the end when he would otherwise give up. What is important to note is that the novel form brings Huxley's natural qualities to a higher development. The precise psychological delineation, the close observation of man alone and in society, the irony, the wide ranging view—everything that distinguishes the essays is intensified by the glow of the creative imagination which the novel arouses in him.

The reason that he has done few novels, and has written those slowly, is because to compose fiction he requires the stimulus of ideas, of hitherto unexplored psychological peculiarities, of new technical tricks. Once stimulated by the possibilities of exploring this or that peculiarity of the psyche (he is working now on a novel dealing with the individual's experience of the past in the present), this or that technical literary device, his imagination begins to create characters, situations, names, and gradually a novel takes shape. The important point to note is that the novel does not occur to him in the form of a story. It is the dramatization of that talking to himself which proceeds at a lower level of excitement in the essays. It is a working model of his inner debate. In his characters he can see what his ideas look like dressed in human form.

But once his imagination is stirred into action, he creates with a firmness of construction, a sureness of form, which, despite his protest,[1] is of a kind only describable as classical. Artists speak of a draughtsman having a sure sense of the direction of a line. In the same way, we feel confident, in reading Huxley's novels, that he knows exactly which way he is going. We may not know ourselves, but we are sure he knows. There is never any danger of a mistake. The line never deviates into meaningless, uncertain darts and flurries. Besides Huxley I can think of only three writers who have the same assured sense of

[1] 'For I have never had the smallest ambition to be a Classic of any kind, whether Neo, Palaeo, Proto or Eo.'— *Vulgarity in Literature.*

direction—Fielding, T. S. Eliot and Molière. In
Molière the assurance might almost be described as
arrogance. His *Don Juan*, for instance, makes one
feel that here is a dramatist who is delightfully cock-
sure of his ability to do anything and get away with
it. It is the confidence of the supreme juggler.

Spend a lifetime circling miscellaneous objects
round your head, and you will eventually be able to
throw in an odd novelty such as a bird-cage or a
jack-boot without getting excited. You will have
reached complete mastery of your art. There is such
a thing as perfection.

Formally, art is only juggling. Huxley, like
Molière, can circle blocks of words round his head
with the arrogant grace of a master juggler. When
you think everything will crash, he adds a glass of
champagne, smiles, and continues, with Olympian
unconcern. It is dazzling. It is intoxicating. It is
perfection. And it is classical, not romantic.

The curious thing is, as every writer knows, that
what may seem to the reader the perfection of controlled and conscious art, has not seemed at all like
that to the author. So much of a novel suggests itself
in the very process of writing. Scenes, characters
and places not originally contemplated seem to spring
from some dark, unexplored store-house of the mind.
I do not doubt that many of the apparently most
carefully planned set-pieces in Huxley's or any other
novelist's works have been impromptus, have suddenly burst into the midst of quite other intentions.
But this does not invalidate terms like balance, control,

direction. Such classical qualities are as intuitive as the romantic ones. They show themselves in the ability to turn the impromptus of the subconscious to good account. Design which, in literature as in the plastic arts, must be learned at the beginning, becomes with much practice, intuitive.

Huxley, congenitally an essayist, has done his most lasting work in fiction. He has declined to stop at what came easily to him. Stimulated by the ' forme au travail rebelle ' of the novel he has produced five books which from their poise, irony and compact strength we feel to be works of bright and enduring beauty.

Chapter 4

MAN ALONE

The greatest, the most important of the arts is living.
Texts and Pretexts.

'If one would live well,' says Huxley in *Do What You Will*, 'one must live completely, with the whole being—with the body and instincts, as well as with the conscious mind.'

This hint of how to achieve the good life, which we have considered in its dramatized form in *Point Counter Point*, is elaborated in *Do What You Will* into a philosophy. Through a series of essays Huxley moves in widening, concentric circles round this central idea. With a wide reference of examples ranging from the talkies to Spinoza, he takes up and examines point after point of man's nature, bringing his argument to a conclusion in his doctrine of life-worship. It is a doctrine at once intellectually sound and practically possible. It stands, in a sense, midway between the life-philosophies proposed by the only two contemporary English writers in any way comparable with Huxley, that is D. H. Lawrence and T. S. Eliot. Huxley's philosophy, like Eliot's, has order, but it is not an order imposed by authority; it has spontaneity, like Lawrence's, but it avoids anarchy.

This philosophy owes something to Lawrence

and Blake for its inspiration; but not everything. Huxley had already felt the inadequacy of his own intellectualism before he began intensively to read these authors. They expressed, possibly over-emphatically, what he had long been aware of. The works of these writers are, as it were, the myths out of which Huxley has drawn the texts for his own more consciously formulated doctrine. He has worked out analytically and intellectually what Lawrence and Blake wrote instinctively and emotionally. Blake's protest against 'the dark Satanic mills' of industrial England was necessary; so too was Lawrence's protest against 'the grey ones' who inhabit that England. No less necessary was the scientific, intellectual justification of their protests which Huxley has supplied. By themselves Lawrence and Blake could only be inspirational forces; they could only be of service to the spiritually gifted. The deplorable effect of Lawrence's teaching on the good of intention but dull of wit is, alas, only too obvious in centres of culture. The majority of the young men and women who read Lawrence with such blind admiration are the worst possible advertisement for him. Only those who already know how to live should be entrusted with the Lawrencian philosophy in the raw. His youthful disciples too often illustrate in their lives a travesty of their master. For such persons a logically argued creed such as that which Huxley provides is far more suitable. Even so, it is open to great misunderstanding, as Huxley is aware :

'. . . in effect,' he says, ' the " Do what thou
wilt " of Thelema was addressed only to " men
that are free, well-born, well-bred, and conver-
sant in honest companies." For the others, restraints from without in the shape of policemen,
from within in the shape of superstitions, will
always be necessary.'

But for a certain class of Englishmen, for those
educated at public-schools, for the convention-bound
English gentleman, the Huxleyan philosophy of life-
worship can be of the greatest service. Were it
adopted, its effect would be to change the archetype
of the practical politician into something like the archetype of those impractical sensitive beings who inhabit the novels of Turgeniev and the tales of Tchehov.
It would produce a revolution in England, perhaps
a revolution in the whole world. England has always
from time to time produced men who were the
very antithesis of the Continental idea of the typical
Englishman. But the shopkeepers have always feared
the poets who lurked in their own breasts and have
for long endeavoured to repress those poets out of
existence. It would be a strange day when the
Englishman was held out as the typical, unreliable,
unpractical artist, and the Russian or the Italian as the
perfect hard-headed business-man, the ideal politician.
And yet Communism and Fascism make it look as
though such a revolution were not so very far ahead.

' The best life-worshippers,' says Huxley, ' are
probably those who have been strictly educated

in Christian or bourgeois morality, in the philosophy of common-sense tempered by religion, and have afterwards revolted against their upbringing. . . . For the well-born young aspirant to a cell in Gargantua's abbey I would recommend the most conventional of gentlemanly and Anglican public-school educations, followed, at the university, by an intensive course of theoretical Pyrrhonism and the practice of all Blake's most subversive precepts. . . . His public-school traditions would bring him honourably and sensibly through the affairs of social life, while his course of Pyrrhonism would have taught him to disregard the restraints imposed by these traditions on his activities as an individual, or colony of individuals.'

Make people happy and they find it easy to be good. Or rather, since it is impossible to *make* people happy, provide conditions favourable to happiness and show people how to be themselves, how to satisfy all their desires in such a way that they avoid the extremes of starvation and of surfeit. The happily married woman finds it easy to avoid committing adultery ; the man who has pleasant, congenial work does not have to take the pledge.

To provide conditions favourable to happiness is the task of society, it is to a large extent outside the powers of the individual. But to be oneself, to develop one's whole character felicitously, is essentially the individual's concern.

Huxley, in *Do What You Will*, is dealing with this

problem. Elsewhere, chiefly in *Proper Studies*, he
has treated of man in society. Here his subject is
man alone.

His practical advice is briefly stated :

> ' The only satisfactory way of existing in the
> modern, highly specialized world is to live with
> two personalities. A Dr. Jekyll that does the
> metaphysical and scientific thinking, that transacts
> business in the city, adds up figures, designs
> machines and so forth. And a natural, spontaneous
> Mr. Hyde to do the physical, instinctive living in
> the intervals of work. The two personalities
> should lead their unconnected lives apart, without
> poaching on one another's activities. Only by
> living discretely and inconsistently can we preserve
> both the man and the citizen, both the intellectual
> and the spontaneous animal being, alive within us.
> The solution may not be very satisfactory ; but it
> is, I believe now (though I once thought differently),
> the best that, in modern circumstances, can be
> devised.'

The common manner of using one's spare time is
not one which would appeal to Huxley, or indeed to
any even moderately cultured and sensitive man or
woman. As generally interpreted the spare time self
of the typical citizen of an industrial country is an
individual who does not, apparently, differ greatly
from his working self. The mechanization which
pervades the one section of his life seems to pervade
also the other. There does not appear to be much

spontaneous, instinctive, animal life about the citizen in the cinema queue, the citizen mooning over his newspaper, the citizen dozing in front of a loud-speaker. Certainly, there is little here to commend itself to the strongly individualized man or woman. But one may question whether these seemingly mechanized amusements are as deficient in vital interest for those who partake of them as they seem. The educated and distinctive individual is probably in error when he attributes to the cinema queues his own dislike for these amusements. The 'Little Man,' who has replaced John Bull as the national symbol, thoroughly enjoys himself at the cinema, gazing at his newspaper, or dozing by the radio. He is far better supplied with excuses for dreamy mindlessness than is, for example, an Albanian tribesman. The latter when he wants to be idle, which is quite as often as does the 'Little Man,' can only smoke his pipe, and sit in the sun. The moralist is tempted to regard this as more natural, more healthily instinctive than dreaming over a newspaper. But is this not some-what anachronistic moralizing? What is instinctive to the pastoral tribesman is by no means instinctive to the industrial worker. It is instinctive for *him* to get home to his radio after his day's work. In doing that he *is* living spontaneously and instinctively. It may be claimed that his habits are merely the result of circumstances, of fashion, of newspaper publicity. But so too are the habits of the Albanian herdsman. Circumstances oblige him to spend his leisure smoking his pipe in mindless vacancy. There is nothing else he can do. If he had a radio, he would enjoy it as much as the industrial worker. In comparison with the difference in the standard of living between the two, the radio is not more unnatural or unspontaneous for the industrial worker than the pipe and cup of coffee for the Albanian. The news-bulletins and lectures of the B.B.C. are about equal to the gossip of the Balkan peasant's coffee-house as an excuse for pleasantly idle rumination.

It is therefore, I think, useless for a moralist like Huxley to cry out against the mechanized, 'creation-saving' amusements of industrial states. These amusements bore and disgust him, and with him many intelligent and sensitive people. But they are genuinely satisfying to the masses. Standing in a cinema queue satisfies the gregarious instinct, and the film itself satisfies the desire for vicarious adventure and romance as well as did the fairy-tales of less mechanized ages.

Where the spare-time life of the 'Little Man' is definitely inferior to the life of the uncivilized peasant is, without doubt, in everything that touches his sexual experiences.

There is no need here to rehearse again what has been said by many psychologists and moralists in the last thirty years on the unsatisfactory state of the sexual life of western Europeans and Americans. The pernicious effects of Puritanism and industrialism are only too well known.

To find evidence of this unsatisfactory state of affairs it is hardly necessary to go outside the family circle. Any one who cares to think frankly and carefully about the private life of his parents, his nearer relatives, cannot fail to discover endless unhappiness, nervous illness and bad temper which had no other cause than a sexual one.

In expounding his philosophy of ' balanced excess ' Huxley should, I think, have concentrated more on this aspect of the life of the contemporary citizen. It is in this field that his principle can be most fruitfully applied. It is here that it proves most valuable as a guide to greater happiness.

The conditions of life in an industrial town obviously do not permit of a woman satisfying her maternal instincts to the same extent as is possible in an agricultural community. Mussolini's campaign for bigger and bigger families may not do much harm to the women of Italy, may not cause much unhappiness, but in England it would be disastrous. For the wife of an industrial worker in London or Glasgow to have a large family will obviously cause the greatest unhappiness. It is highly regrettable that this should be so, but until a communistic state arises, the small family remains unavoidable. That being so, the techniques of contraception and abortion are necessary. In addition to that, men and women require to know more about their own psychologies, to understand better their instincts, if they are to be happy. Such knowledge must be scientifically, realistically stated, not in terms of a theology of which an outside authority alone has the control. Only so can the individual master his own life.

Now it is because Huxley's life-worship philosophy is based on the observable facts of human behaviour, and is stated in as scientifically accurate terms as possible, that it is so valuable.

Here it will be advisable to give a summary of this philosophy.

To begin with, certain basic principles have to be established. Huxley applies to man's inner life the methods of the physical sciences. What, he asks, are the observable, undeniable facts? What is the data with which the nature of man presents us?

Clearly, the only thing we can actually know by direct experience is our inner life. It may be that the external world does not exist at all. But to our human perceiving apparatus it seems that the world does exist. There is no getting away from that inner conviction, and equally there is no getting behind it. ' The only facts of which we have direct knowledge are psychological facts.'

Further :

' One fact cannot be more of a fact than another. Our psychological experiences are all equally facts. . . . No psychological experience is " truer," so far as we are concerned, than any other. For even if one should correspond more closely to things in themselves as perceived by some hypothetical non-human being, it would be impossible for us to discover what it was.'

Having established the premisses that truth is internal and that one psychological fact cannot be more or less true than another such fact, it is possible to discuss the two chief types of religion, polytheism and monotheism.

To say that polytheism is false and monotheism is true, is shown to be a meaningless statement. These two doctrines are the rationalizations of two different interior human experiences, neither of which can be considered, for the reasons given, as truer than the other. In certain circumstances, it is observable that men are disposed to see an essential unity in the universe. In other circumstances, they see only disunity. In the one case monotheism is the appropriate religion, in the other, polytheism. The polytheistic system of the Greeks, is, for Huxley, preferable to the monotheism of the Hebrews, because, he says, ' Their pantheon contained representatives of every vital activity—representatives of the body and the instincts as well as of the spirit, of the passionate energies as well as of the reason, of the self-regarding as well as of the altruistic tendencies of human nature.'

On the other hand, ' Contemporary monotheism is an expression of our excessive love for that abstract knowledge of the general and the uniform which enables us to predict and organize and do many other useful things, but gives us, alas! no sustenance by which we may live.'

Abstract and generalized knowledge—the knowledge of science—gives man power over the world. Concrete and multifarious gods give man an enlargement of himself as a man, but have no effect on the universe. The modern world has chosen the former.

But do we want to go on chosing it? Is it not time we gave plain human nature a chance? In short:

'Which is the more valuable for life—the unity-feeling with its various religious or philosophical rationalizations, or the diversity-feeling with *its* attendant doctrines?'

Christianity and industrialism, which are products of the unity-feeling, have discouraged every aspect of life but the mental and the spiritual. That a life so lived was incomplete has been vaguely and almost unconsciously realized by many people, among them being those who have attempted to re-start village crafts, to revive the folk-music and folk-art of England, even by those who go on hikes. All these things are a protest against mechanized life. The weakness of these movements is that they are self-conscious. The folk-lore enthusiast and the hiker, in making their protest, feel slightly in the wrong about it. They are a minority, and to be in a minority always produces an uneasy self-awareness. Further, these things are only temporary and partial escapes. They must inevitably be felt as side-shows to the main part of existence, and such a feeling about any activity detracts greatly from its value.

'To live,' says Huxley, 'the soul must be in intimate contact with the world, must assimilate it through all the channels of sense and desire, thought and feeling, which nature has provided for the purpose. . . . Close up enough of these channels, cut off enough of its nourishment, and the starved soul dies.'

And with the death of the soul comes, of course, the birth of the perfect Citizen, the obeyer of the law. It is remarkable how, in daily life, even the most intelligent and sensitive of one's acquaintances tend to assume that one's function as a citizen is the most important part of life. Time and again, friends enquire, apparently with interest and sympathy, ' And how are you getting on with your job ? '

Slightly startled, and recalled as from far away, I need a minute or two to think of some suitable reply which will not lower my prestige as an efficient citizen. It is not always easy, and often I am tempted to be quite honest and reply, ' Well, really I never think about it.' And indeed, out of office hours, I do not. At the moment when these sympathetic enquiries are addressed to me, the most important thing in my mind is probably some simple event of one's domestic or sexual or intellectual life which has been peculiarly satisfying. But to speak of such things to the efficient citizen is to invite either pity, contempt or, more likely, complete incomprehension.

Huxley has no doubt, and I have no doubt either, that the diversity feeling is the more valuable for life.

' If men are ever to rise again from the depths into which they are now descending,' he says, ' it will only be with the aid of a new religion of life. And since life is diverse, the new religion

will have to have many Gods. Many; but since
the individual man is an unity in his various
multiplicity, also one. It will have to be Dionysian
and Panic as well as Apollonian; Orphic as well
as rational; not only Christian, but Martial and
Venerean too; Phallic as well as Minervan or
Jehovahistic. It will have to be all, in a word,
that human life actually is, not merely the symbolical
expression of one of its aspects.'

It is in a long essay on Pascal, rich in ideas, that
Huxley propounds the main part of his doctrine.
He first of all shows that man is not a consistent
being, that he is now one thing, now another. But
despite this, ' Men,' he says, ' do not want to admit
that they are in fact what they are—each one a colony
of separate individuals.' And yet it is a matter of
experience that ' even the most ardent positivist is
sometimes carried away by a wave of mystical
emotion. Even the most frenzied absolute-hunters,
aesthetes and idealists must compromise with the
gross world of relativity and practice to the extent of
eating, taking shelter from the weather, behaving at
least conventionally enough to keep out of the
clutches of the police.'

Women, of course, have always delighted in draw-
ing the attention of the philosophers to these material
necessities. The search for the absolute has always
seemed to them a slightly comic activity, if an en-
gagingly pathetic one.

But man, as Huxley says, has always insisted on

'being *either* Pascal *or* Voltaire, *either* Podsnap *or* Keats.'

Huxley's proposal is that we should abandon these attempts at self-consistency. The scientific study of our inner life shows that we are naturally diverse, that our outward circumstances, our physical condition, the ebb and flow of sexual desire, all conspire to make now one feeling predominate, now another. In the past men have attempted to suppress all feelings except those which they had been taught to regard as 'true,' as corresponding to their 'better self.' But regarded realistically, we cannot consider one psychological state to be truer or better than another. Instead, then, of seeking to be consistent, let us accept our natural diversity, and base our conduct of life upon that. Since diverse we naturally are, we cannot surely be wrong in following nature.

'The life-worshipper's philosophy is comprehensive. As a manifold and discontinuous being, he is in a position to accept all the partial and apparently contradictory syntheses constructed by other philosophers. . . . There is really no question of any of these philosophies being true or false. The psychological state called joy is no truer than the psychological state called melancholy. . . . Each is a primary fact of experience. And since one psychological state cannot be truer than another, since all are equally facts, it follows that the rationalization of one state cannot be truer than the rationalization of another.'

This is reminiscent of Blake's theory of ' states ' of sin or righteousness, etc.—which visit the individual, but for which he is not actually responsible. There are obvious objections to this theory, some of which Huxley has himself considered in *Texts and Pretexts*. One might point simply to the fact of memory as showing that even if a man is nothing but a series of states, nevertheless these states are connected and built up into a more or less coherent whole which is never the same from one individual to another.

Orthodox moralists will object to Huxley's philosophy that putting it into practice would result in the disintegration, the absolute falling to pieces of most persons. Held in shape by some sort of subservience to the Christian doctrine, by commonsense ethics, most, it will be argued, would have no sort of guide to conduct if they seriously attempted to live as variously as their natures might incline them.

And of course, this is to some extent true. Some persons will always have so weak a sense of values, that, without an externally imposed law, they will drift, at the mercy of whatever impinges upon them, incapable of forming a law of their own.

Huxley's reply to this objection I have already quoted. He says further :

' In the case, moreover, of a sincere life-worshipper, his religion is a guarantee against swinishness. For swinishness is not a manifestation of life, but a blasphemy against it. Thus, swinish gluttony and swinish drunkenness are devices for lowering vitality, not enhancing it. Swinish promiscuity is not an expression of that spontaneous desire which ' plants fruits of life and beauty ' in human personality. . . . Swinish avarice and covetousness limit vitality, canalizing its flow in a narrow and filthy channel. Cruelty, which is occasionally appropriate and necessary and is then life-enhancing, is life-limiting and life-destroying when it is turned into a habitual re-action, when it becomes, in a word, swinish cruelty.'

This last sentence is particularly instructive. For when Huxley says that all manifestations of life are godlike, and every element in human nature has a divine right to expression, the objection that at once suggests itself is that in such case many of those qualities which Huxley has so severely criticized should be allowed to exist. If we feel puritanical, may we not express that side of our nature ? May we not also be sadistic, masochistic, parsimonious, slothful, wrathful, covetous, concupiscent ?

The objection is, however, really a purely formal one. Certain elements in human nature, which we have been accustomed to think natural and unchanging, can clearly be shown to be the result of economic circumstances. Thus puritanism corresponds to the northern countries of Europe where securing a liveli-hood is a sterner task than in the south. The

Sabbatarianism, as well as the parsimony of the Scotch, for instance, is undoubtedly a product of the barrenness and poverty of their land.

In respect of certain other qualities of human nature which we have been accustomed to call vices, it is not difficult to distinguish between those which narrow the individual into himself and those which enlarge his contact with the world. There is not much doubt which is the way to greater happiness. For those who believe in a future life, and consider that they have a soul to be saved, withdrawal into the self may be necessary. But for those who live only in this life, expansion is the rule.

When Huxley says that cruelty is occasionally necessary, he is expressing as a generalization what must be a fact of personal experience for those who can consider themselves without prejudice. A degree of cruelty is above all necessary in the sexual life of healthy men and women. The man desires to express his dominance by inflicting a measure of pain, and the woman equally desires to feel pain, desires to be dominated, to be a sacrifice. It is particularly in respect of this need for cruelty that the sexual life of the 'Little Man' is inferior to that of the peasant. The 'Little Man' has been taught to look with horror upon cruelty. So strongly has he been conditioned in this matter that he can even be persuaded into parting with his money to suppress sports involving the death of small and useless animals. And he will even finance propaganda against medical experiments which are of direct benefit to himself. This aversion to cruelty does not, however, prevent the ' Little Man ' rushing into a war for the extermination of his fellow creatures. It seems clear that the sadistic instinct in man is so deeply embedded, that it has roots stretching back for so many thousands of years into the early origins of the human race, that it is useless to try and exterminate it. If the expression of this instinct is refused in one direction it will break out in another. You cannot have both the suppression of cruelty to animals and world peace. It cannot be denied that it is a remarkable coincidence that the world's most disastrous war should have followed the period of greatest extension of the humanitarian doctrine. I sometimes think that a Society for the Encouragement of Cruelty to Animals or an International League for the Propagation of Bull-fighting might pacify the world quicker than the League of Nations.

I suggest this because it is probably easier for most men to work off their sadistic instincts on animals than on their wives. Actually, it would be better if they could be taught to take the latter course. But the wives too will need educating. Few will admit, even to themselves, what are in fact their natural desires.

Equally, as Huxley implies, men and women will need educating not to behave swinishly in these matters.

'Indeed,' he says, 'any course of behaviour pursued to the exclusion of all the other possible courses open to a normally diverse personality is obviously, according to our standards, immoral, because it limits and distorts the manifestations of life. In the eyes of the life-worshipper such exclusiveness is a sin. His doctrine of moderation demands that one excess shall be counterbalanced by another. To continue on principle or by force of habit in one course is to destroy that vital equilibrium whose name is virtue, and run into immorality.'

In nothing is this more evidently true than in the sexual life. To continue to profess love, long after it has died, to persist in chastity at the command of some external authority when all the instinctive desires are against it—can anything be more truly immoral than these courses of conduct?

The life-worshipper, says Huxley, ' will be by turns excessively passionate and excessively chaste.' It is indeed the only satisfactory way to live, because it follows the natural physiological rise and fall of desire in the human organism. In man as much as in woman desire wells up and subsides with a more or less regular periodicity. When the tide is at flood, all barriers should be removed. When the tide is at ebb, no attempt should be made to call it back.

This principle is equally valid for other aspects of daily life. Most women, for instance, are happier living in alternate luxury and stringent economy than on a steady level of moderate comfort. The ' model husband ' is such an unsatisfactory husband because he does not realize this. Equally, the good housewife does not realize that affection is better preserved by occasional frivolities than by stolidly being ' a good wife.'

The fundamental assumptions of the life-worshipper may be summed up as follows :

(1) He believes that life is valuable in itself.

(2) He believes that the purpose of living is to live.

(3) Without contrast and diversity life is inconceivable.

(4) Therefore he believes in having as much contrast and diversity as possible.

The life-worshipper will be ' at times a positivist and at times a mystic ; derisively sceptical and full of faith. He will live light-hearted or earnest, and when the sick Pascalian mood is upon him, correct his frivolities and ambitions with the thought of death. In a word, he will accept each of his selves, as it appears in his consciousness as his momentarily true self. Each and all he will accept—even the bad, even the mean and suffering, even the death-worshipping and naturally Christian souls. He will accept, he will live the life of each, excessively.'

*　　*　　*

Opposition to Huxley's system of morals is to be expected from the Christians. And from what one knows of the different Churches one may expect a greater opposition from the Protestant than the Roman Catholic. Whether this is actually the case or not it is difficult to state precisely. I can only give a few typical judgments.

For example, I have heard a Catholic priest say, speaking of *Brave New World*—'Aldous Huxley? He is on the side of the angels by now. We know that.'

On the other hand the German Catholic Encyclopaedia, ' Der Grosse Herder,' dismisses Huxley with the remark : ' Geistvoller Skeptiker und Zyniker der modernen Krisenliteratur; ohne wirkliche Tiefe.' But the capacity of this ' reference work for knowledge and life ' to judge of ' real depth ' may be estimated from the fact that it rates Huxley's short stories above his novels.

More interesting is the fact that in the British Museum Reading Room the only two works dealing with Huxley are respectively a Protestant and a Roman Catholic study of his moral philosophy.

The Protestant work, a pamphlet published by the Society for Propagating Christian Knowledge, is entitled *The Undisciplined Life* and is by a Mr. Roger Lloyd. As the title of this pamphlet will at once indicate, its argument is based on a misunderstanding. And the misunderstanding is likely to be permanent, because Mr. Lloyd does not appreciate that the premiss from which he argues is entirely different from that of Aldous Huxley. A quotation will make this at once clear :

' He has a blind spot,' says Mr. Lloyd, ' an incapacity which makes him incapable of understanding. That blind spot, I believe, can be traced to the fact that he always appears to conceive of religion as being subjective, egocentric, as starting with man and his circumstances, and deducing the Deity from the human angle. But, surely, in any of the great religions the precise opposite is the truth. True religion takes its origin from God, and unless it is believed to start in this way it ceases to be religion.'

In that last sentence is the whole difference. Huxley has shown that the religious sentiment *is* simply a psychological fact and that man can never know whether this sentiment originates in or corresponds with any external Being, Force, God or whatever one chooses to call this hypothetical element.

The unbridgeable gulf between Mr. Lloyd and Huxley is further indicated when Mr. Lloyd says that the aim of the Christian art of life is ' the fullness of communion with the Unseen.'

One may, of course, explain one's mystical emotions as union with the Christian God, but as Huxley points out, Buddhists, Moslems, Hindus and cultured modernists all explain the same emotion in different ways. And there is no means of knowing whether one is truer than the other. Hence the only possible course, if one cares at all for such truth as is obtainable, is to take the mystical emotion as a fact and leave it at that, along with all the other facts of human nature.

Mr. Lloyd claims that 'the Christian moral tradition stands inflexibly opposed' to Huxley's philosophy. Clearly, however, he cannot speak for the whole of

Christianity, since Mr. Gerald Vann, O.P., in his book *On Being Human: St. Thomas and Mr. Aldous Huxley*, has something more than a good word for the life-worshipper's creed.

Father Vann, who is a Dominican priest, is a contributor to *Blackfriars*, the most advanced of intellectual Catholic publications, so that his views are doubtless not those of the ordinary parish priest. Nevertheless the book bears the official Roman Catholic censor's *imprimatur*.

Consequently it is somewhat surprising to read :

' Yet Mr. Huxley considers his thesis opposed to the Christian ideal, opposed to monotheism of any sort, whereas the purpose of this essay has been precisely to try and show its identity with Christianity and with the Catholic doctor, St. Thomas Aquinas.'

Mr. Vann's essay is much better written than Mr. Lloyd's ; it is the product of a far more deeply cultured mind, a mind which could not so misunderstand a writer's intention as Mr. Lloyd does. The Catholic writer understands well enough, that far from advocating an ' undisciplined life ' Huxley is out for a better discipline than existing institutions can, in his opinion, offer. And having understood that, he tries to convince Huxley and the reader of Huxley that the life-worshipper's creed can be better practised inside the Church than outside.

' Mr. Huxley,' says this writer, ' is on the side of the humans, and human nature, poor thing, has been so badgered and browbeaten and bothered during the course of the last several centuries, that it is good to find so potent a defender of its honour joining forces at least in this respect with thomism and with the issues of the supernatural principles of Catholicism. For Catholicism the creed and thomism the philosophy, whatever may justly be charged against this or that individual, have always defended it. And in both of them the life-worshipper's faith is brought to completion; in both of them (for thomism is here the glad debtor of the faith) man finds a fulfilment immeasurably more excessive in Mr. Huxley's sense than a pagan polytheism could dream of. . . .'

*   *   *

I said earlier that the philosophy of balanced excess could be most valuably applied in the field of love, and in the course of analysing that philosophy I have endeavoured to give concrete examples of what I meant. Before we conclude this examination of *Do What You Will*, it would be useful to consider the rather brief essay in which Huxley deals specifically with the sexual life.

Summarizing the argument, what Huxley says is this : Love is the resultant of two forces : the one a more or less unchanging group of passions, instincts and desires, and the other the widely varying group of laws, ideals, conventions and beliefs which have arisen in all times and all places.

At the present time, he contends, there are two

hostile conceptions of love struggling for survival in the Western world. One is the conception gradually evolved in the nineteenth century out of the Christian dread of passion and the romantic worship of passion. The ideal of this conception is a perpetual, exclusive monogamy.

Opposed to this is the realistic conception which arose, ultimately, out of the war. It was, to begin with, a theory called in to justify existing behaviour. Later, it became the cause of new behaviour in the post-war generation. This new conception ' recognizes the diversity of love, not merely in the social mass from age to age, but from individual to contemporary individual, according to the dosage of the different instincts with which each is born, and the upbringing he has received. . . . Love has ceased to be the rather fearful, mysterious thing it was, and become a perfectly normal, almost commonplace, activity— an activity for many young people, especially in America, of the same nature as dancing or tennis— a sport, a recreation, a pastime. For those who hold this conception of love, liberty and toleration are prime necessities. A strenuous offensive against the old taboos and repressions is everywhere in progress.'

Both systems have defects. The nineteenth-century Christian-romantic pattern was bad because of its intolerance to those who could not fit in with it. The new conception is bad in so far as it makes love too easy. ' Too much enjoyment blunts the fine point of seldom pleasure. Unrestrained indulgence kills

not merely passion, but, in the end, even amusement.'
Hence, this fashion in love is not likely to last long.
It will be found that restraints are necessary. The
question then is, what restraints will be chosen?
Traditional morality will no doubt continue to play a
part, but Huxley suggests other and less transcendental, more human restraints are likely to be called in.
These will be 'of a more fundamental, less artificial
nature—emotional, not intellectual. The impulse is
to be restrained from promiscuous manifestations
because, if it were not, promiscuity would " harden
all within and petrify the feeling." The restraint is of
the same personal nature as the impulse. The conflict
is between a part of the personality and the personality as an organized whole. . . . This doctrine has
several great advantages over previous systems of
inward restraint. It does not postulate the existence
of any transcendental, non-human entity. . . . People
will cease to be interested in unknowable absolutes;
but they will never lose interest in their own personalities.'

It is difficult to see why this should be regarded
as an ignoble conception of love, though many have
found it so, whether expounded by Huxley or by
D. H. Lawrence. When Huxley speaks of 'the beautiful and humorous, the rather absurd but sacred,
but sublime and marvellous world of carnal passion
and tenderness,' he is surely only describing in quite un-
exaggerated terms a universal experience. Hundreds
do not recognize it because of that deep terror of
the sexual life which is one of the worst products

of the Christian-romantic conception. The quiet, unemphatic way in which Huxley writes of these things is one of the characteristics that must be most alarming to his older readers. Most of them are so full of shame and terror, they cannot understand why others do not feel the same. Most nicely-brought-up middle-class women, for instance, are quite unable to speak of their sexual life even to their doctor. And the most regrettable fact of all is that such people have completely lost faith in the possibility of the heroic devotion and lasting faithfulness which the Christian-romantic mode of love did sometimes produce. Instead, they are left merely with the taboos of that conception. These taboos are barriers which leak ; they do not exert enough pressure to drive up a fountain, they merely get in the way, for the water trickles through slowly, wastefully and muddily. Equally deficient is the flat realism which removes with one hasty decision all barriers, future as well as past.

' Only,' says Huxley, ' a new mythology of nature, such as, in modern times, Blake, Robert Burns, and Lawrence have defined it, an untrans-cendental and (relatively speaking) realistic myth-ology of Energy, Life, and Human Personality, will provide, it seems to me, the inward resistances necessary to turn sexual impulse into love, and provide them in a form which the critical intelli-gence of Post-Nietzschean youth can respect. By means of such a conception a new fashion in love may be created, more healthful and elegant, than any seen among men since the days of remote and pagan antiquity.'

Such a new fashion in love is, it seems to me, gradually arising in the first generation of post-war English men and women. By this I mean those now between twenty and thirty, for they are the first generation to reach maturity which really did not know the war. Any one who is twenty-five now was only nine when the war ended. At that age the only effects which the war could have would be physiological ones due to inferior food, disturbed rest owing to air-raids, and so forth. Events which shake the whole of society hardly touch a child under the age of fourteen. A remarkable idealism is noticeable in this first post-war generation. It pours itself into Communism, Fascism, poetry, the rediscovery of romantic love, even into patriotism, for Communism has made it possible for the intelligent to be patriotic once again. 'You that love England' writes a revolutionary poet, Cecil Day Lewis, 'do you not hear the entrance of a new theme?' The new theme is Communism. But for some the new theme is also Fascism, is also sexual faithfulness—a new fashion in love.

*   *   *

Objections can be made to Huxley's principle of balanced excess. Some of them I have dealt with. I will advance one more, but rather in the form of a question than as a counter-argument. Huxley takes large sections of mankind to task because they have sought to unify their lives on the basis of one principle, to be, what he calls, ' monsters of consistency.' He objects to this on the ground that it is against life, against nature, for, he says, man is naturally multifarious. Well, is he? or rather, are all men? To simplify one's life, to build it round a single core, gives a man power over himself and, still more, power over others, over his surrounding world. And some psychologists maintain that the power urge is as fundamental in man as the urge to reproduction. Huxley is obviously himself of the multifarious type. For him, to know is the greatest good. For others, it is to do. And to do, to act, a man must make himself into a sharp and strong machine, must concentrate, unify his forces, must prune everything in the interests of his one most deeply desired aim. To be a man of action means that you take other men and women as the medium of your art. And that means intolerance. That means forcing your own will on others, commanding them to simplify, to become part of the machine. It will not do for a sculptor to exercise tolerance towards his stone; it has to be cut the way he wants it. Just so the man of power cuts life into the shape he wills; he is, in short, of necessity intolerant.

For many, the life-worshipper's creed is, no doubt, too lacking in moral props and restraints. It is felt to impose too great a strain on the individual. But for those who are capable of effort, it is a creed which will not seem wanting in discipline. Many, surely, will agree with Huxley when he says :

> ' And yet the life-worshipper is also, in his own way a man of principles and consistency. To live intensely—that is his guiding principle. His diversity is a sign that he consistently tries to live up to his principles ; for the harmony of life—of the single life that persists as a gradually changing unity through time—is a harmony built up of many elements. The unity is mutilated by the suppression of any part of the diversity. A fugue has need of all its voices. Even in the rich counterpoint of life each separate small melody plays its indispensable part. The diapason closes full in man. In *man*.'

For men living, as we feel ourselves to be, upon the brink of war and disaster, the philosophy of life-worship is not an ignoble one. It may even lend a certain dignity and passion to lives almost certain to be short.

Chapter 5

MAN IN SOCIETY

One thing alone is absolutely certain of the future : that our Western societies will not long persist in their present state.—*Proper Studies.*

IN *Do What You Will* Huxley is concerned with the way a man can build his life ; he considers man, so far as possible alone. He follows Christian theory in that he clearly thinks that man has a soul to be saved, the difference being that for him the saving must be done in this world. Huxley has never ceased to be a salvationist, that salvationist which he discerned within himself—and with what dismay !—at the very beginning of his career. ' Intellectually a Voltairian, emotionally a Bunyanite.' He is still that. Fortunately he has never succeeded in suppressing the Bunyanite, but has taken the more profitable course of putting his salvationist emotions at the service of his intellect.

But man does not exist in a vacuum. ' Men are also citizens.' In *Proper Studies* Huxley deals less with man alone than with man in society. His subjects are education, the idea of equality, democracy, religion, eugenics. Lawrence criticized *Proper Studies* for being professorial, and for its ' dry-mindedness.' It is a criticism which may be admitted. The book has nothing like the enthusiastic vigour and movement of *Do What You Will,* where the thought develops symphonically towards what Huxley very aptly calls a ' Musical conclusion.' Whereas *Do What You Will* is rich, coloured, warm, even passionate, the dry intellectuality of *Proper Studies* sticks through the prose like bones.

This is perhaps no objection if we keep strictly to what the author sets out to do in *Proper Studies*. These essays, he says, were intended as an attempt to methodize the ideas which he had derived, from reading and observation, about certain aspects of social and individual life. The book is, then, primarily a work of self-clarification. It may, as the author hopes, help others to sort out their ideas. But from its nature, the book's ideal reader is its writer. What is method for him may not be method for other readers. There remains too the fact that clearness and method are hardly ever satisfactory by themselves. ' Sweetness and light ' are all very well, but most people require a little warmth, before they will even begin to look for the light. And there is not much warmth in *Proper Studies*.

This lack of warmth is perhaps due to the fact that Huxley has, as he says, drawn largely upon other writers for his materials. It is this which gives the book in places the air of a piece of précis writing— admirably lucid, but, like boiled water, not very exhilarating. Ideas of one's own which one has later found expressed at length in other writers, can with difficulty be presented as freshly and vividly as if one had never read the other writers. This is what has happened in much of *Proper Studies*. Huxley says that he found many of his own vague notions set down and documented in the work of Vilfredo Pareto, the Italian economist and sociologist. The result is that in Huxley's book the hand of Pareto has left its mark here and there, so that the prose does not move with its usual brilliance. It is as though little bits of Pareto stuck out and would not be digested. The form may be Huxley's, but the ideas seem sometimes a little insecure inside the form.

Properly to read Pareto's three-volumed *Trattato di Sociologia Generale* requires great strength of will and moral purpose. It is a formidable book. Fortunately one can get some idea of what Pareto has to say from G. H. Bousquet's *Vilfredo Pareto : Sa vie et son œuvre*, or the same author's *Précis de Sociologie d'après Vilfredo Pareto*. There is also a pamphlet translated from Bousquet under the title *The Work of Vilfredo Pareto*, published by the Sociological Press, Liverpool, 1928. This is the only English book on the subject I have been able to discover.

Pareto's method, perhaps even more than Pareto's ideas, appears to have had considerable influence over Huxley in the composition of *Proper Studies*. What that method is may be sufficiently gathered from a passage in the Italian writer's speech on the occasion of his Jubilee in 1917, at Lausanne University, where he was professor.

'It was,' he says, ' at the urging of the desire to add to my investigations into political economy an indispensable complement, and under the inspiration of the example of the natural sciences, that I was led to compose my Traité de Sociologie, the sole purpose of which—the sole purpose, I repeat—is to seek the experimental reality by applying to the social sciences methods that have met the test in physics, chemistry, astronomy, biology and other sciences like them.'

'The experimental reality.' That is what appeals to Huxley. We saw in *Do What You Will* how he was always solicitous for the observable, the experimental reality in human nature. Find that reality and fit your philosophy to it, is his guiding principle. In this he follows the reverse procedure to most philosophers who, beginning with a wish, construct a theory to satisfy that wish, and only then look for evidence in the observable world to justify their wish-fulfilment theory.

Pareto then, in his sociology, looks for the permanent, unchanging elements in man as a social being. On this basis he evolved his distinction of 'residues' and 'derivations.'

The constant part of social facts Pareto calls 'residues.' These are sentiments, tendencies and so forth. The varying parts—the rationalizations, the theories, etc.—he calls 'derivations.'

As an example of 'residue' and 'derivation' he gives religion. Religious exaltation is in all countries and at all times much the same, but the theological derivations vary enormously. It is a point which Huxley too has made a number of times.

Man in society, says Pareto, performs non-logical acts which he claims to justify by vague rationalizations, and which are based on certain fundamental instincts and constant sentiments.

Further, man elaborates or accepts theories and doctrines ' non-logico-experimental,' because they reflect certain tendencies.

Thus, contrary to what is generally believed, men do not act on the authority of certain theories, but they have a certain state of mind which on the one hand drives them to action, and on the other makes them seek for theories, for allegedly logical explanations of their course of action.

The other important influence in *Proper Studies* is a work called *Les Paralogismes du Rationalisme*, an essay on the theory of knowledge by a French professor of philosophy, M. Louis Rougier.

The object of this work—I translate from the author's introduction—is ' to study the arguments by which rationalism claims to justify the belief in the existence of necessary truths, independent of the mind and of nature. It aims at showing that these arguments are devoid of any authentic value. To that end, it exposes the paralogisms which the former conceal and the psychological illusions which have given them birth. To prove that a doctrine is false is not sufficient: it is necessary to show why men have been led to believe it true. Only thus may the error at the root be for ever expelled.'

Here too it is evident that there is a frame of mind which would strongly appeal to Huxley. The exposing of psychological illusions is one of his most congenial occupations.

These two thinkers, then, Pareto and Rougier, permeate *Proper Studies*. I do not propose to make any attempt at tracking down which half of a sentence comes from Pareto and which from Rougier. Such a task, while it will no doubt be one day undertaken by one of those ' scientific ' students of literature whom Huxley so admirably derides, seems to me impossible. It is so because the ideas of these two writers have been assimilated into a mind already rich with its own ideas, because their thoughts have been so completely taken into the texture of another mind that they have, scientifically and precisely, become part of that mind. Hence when Huxley writes on sociological themes he may be restating an idea of Pareto's, or one of his own. It is impossible to tell. It is impossible for him to tell.

A system of thought is not made piecemeal, it grows. It is at once like and unlike what it has grown from. Hence the ultimate futility of all attempts at tracking down 'influences.' *Proper Studies* is not just the *Trattato di Sociologia Generale* and the *Paralogismes du Rationalisme* restated. It is a work which has been fed by these works, but is itself different from what it feeds on. The value of knowing what has fed *Proper Studies* is that thus Huxley will help us to understand Pareto; and to know Pareto will explain Huxley. Having, by comparison, more completely understood both writers than we could if either were taken alone, we shall be in a better position to examine intelligently what they have to say.

It is, actually, fairly easy to lodge objections to a number of statements in *Proper Studies* and to other political reflections of Huxley's in *Do What You Will, Beyond the Mexique Bay*, and *Jesting Pilate* which I shall deal with later. So far as the present book is concerned, it is very likely that, given more space, Huxley could adequately reply to certain of one's criticisms. But others could not be so easily disposed of. And the reason for this weakness is partly that, as he frankly admits, he is not qualified by training to discuss in detail existing social organizations, and partly because, not being naturally politically minded,[1] he is apt to accept uncritically notions which in any other field of human activity he would subject to more severe testing.

'I have tried,' says Huxley in his introduction, ' to give an account, in the most general terms, and in regard to only a few selected aspects of life, of what is. In the light of what is and of what, therefore, might be, I have tried in certain cases to show what ought to be. To be more specific, I have studied first of all certain aspects of individual human nature, and having reached certain conclusions about the individual, I have gone on to consider existing and possible future institutions in the light of these conclusions. . . . A knowledge of human nature provides us with a standard by which to judge existing institutions and all proposals

---

[1] ' But when I am honest with myself, I have to admit that I don't care two pins about political principles.'—*Jesting Pilate.*

for their reform.   Given the individual, we are able
to deduce the desirable institution.'

This is, as Huxley points out, the method of the
political philosophers of the eighteenth century.   Our
present institutions are based on their philosophizing,
and since our present institutions are so very imperfect,
as they manifestly are, we ought surely to be very
suspicious of this method of deducing social forms.
But, says Huxley, it was not the logic of the eighteenth-
century philosophers which was wrong, it was the
premisses from which they started, which were based
on a false conception of human psychology.   Our
present psychological ideas may not be perfect, but
they are at least much nearer the truth than were those
of the *philosophes*.   Hence our deductions should be
much nearer the truth than theirs were.

Huxley then proceeds to criticize the psychological
conceptions of such writers as Babeuf, Rousseau,
Helvétius, Locke, Descartes—which conceptions of
human nature he describes as ' wholly fabulous.'

Now, since the democratic institutions of the nineteenth century were very largely based on the theories
of the eighteenth, it is difficult to believe that those
theories rested on a ' wholly fabulous ' idea of human
nature.   Our democratic institutions may be imperfect, but they have at least worked for a century or so,
and have propagated themselves all over the world.
Had they been devised to fit a ' wholly fabulous ' man,
their divergence from reality would have prevented
them from working at all.

If one takes the remark of Locke that man is ' by nature free, equal and independent ' simply as a statement of absolute fact, as though it were a statement in physics or chemistry, then of course it is untrue.   And in his examination of the idea of equality Huxley does take such statements in such a way.   The thinking is, as Lawrence so very aptly says, ' dry-minded.'   With a perverse obstinacy, and against the natural fluidity of his mind, Huxley uses an almost pompous logic towards these eighteenth-century philosophers.   He limits his vision to the words in front of him.   He recognizes that the equalitarian philosophy was a wish-fulfilment philosophy, but does not take the obvious step of enquiring why the *philosophes* should have wanted man to be ' free, equal and independent.'

It is difficult to get at the truth if one takes words and theories in a vacuum, without the earth from which they grew.   Along with intellectual abstractions it is necessary, surely, to accept the atmosphere of their age, everything in fact which produced them.

Man is never simply what he is at any given moment; he is also what he thinks he ought to be.   He is not simply existing achievement, he is also effort towards future, and different, achievement.

The social injustices of decaying feudalism in the eighteenth century, things like the Calas and Sirven affairs, the restrictions of human liberty, the inequalities, gave rise to such profound dissatisfactions in sensitive and thoughtful men, they could not but desire something different. And the something different they desired was liberty, equality, inde-

pendence. They did not really want these things as
absolutes, they simply wanted more of them than they
had got. But, as Huxley points out, ' men are not
content merely to desire ; they like to have a logical
or pseudo-logical justification for their desires.'

And the accepted, the most widely approved way
of finding a logical justification for your desires in the
eighteenth century was the deductive method employed by Descartes and the rest. You assumed that
every one knew what man was, because there was the
Bible to tell you how man had been created and so
forth, and if that was not sufficient, there was Aristotle.
It never occurred to any one to make such ' enquiries
into human faculty ' as Galton so profitably employed
his time upon. Buffon might have done something of
the kind, but Buffon was afraid of the Church and the
King, especially after he had got into trouble because
his account of the world did not agree with Genesis.

Under the dictatorship of the Church and of the
King you could not say that the existing enslavement
of men was all wrong. But you could say that man
was by nature free, equal and independent, and that
he had fallen from his happy condition owing to his
education. It is not suggested that the *philosophes*
consciously did this. It is simply that the material
conditions of the time made it impossible for them
directly to attack the manifest ills of decaying feudalism. Even Voltaire was at great pains to keep on
the right side of the Court. These material conditions which strongly discouraged the scientific
investigation of man (because it always disagreed

either with God or the King) necessarily obliged the philosophers to keep to the only other method of discussing the universe—the deductive one, which already in any case had the authority of Plato and Aristotle behind it.

This deductive reasoning, then, was the only means available for speculation about what was and what ought to be. Given the desire for more freedom, and equality, and a hatred of existing ecclesiastical, royal and noble privilege as the motive force, the impossibility of questioning the Biblical and Aristotelian idea of man, as a limiting condition, and deductive logic as the means, it seems to me inevitable that the sociologists of the eighteenth century should have roundly declared that reason is the same in all men and that all men are naturally free and equal.

When Babeuf, or Helvétius, or any one else made such statements he was, if you like, expressing a wish fulfilment. He was stating as facts what was really his idea of what ought to be the facts. And such reasoning was accepted because everywhere men felt that privilege, the feudal caste system was too monstrous to go on any longer, everywhere men felt that they *ought to be* free, equal and independent. Thus the conception of human nature held by the eighteenth-century philosophers was not 'wholly fabulous' because people thought, and still think, part of the time, that man ought to be equal, free, and independent. The conception was certainly partly fabulous, because it took as the whole man what was in fact only part of man. Man is what he is and also what he thinks he ought to be. He is acts and faith. The realistic psychology of the Catholic Church was based on the acts and ignored the faith. The psychology of the eighteenth century, and the consequent political institutions of the nineteenth century, were based on the faith and ignored the acts. Faith will often create its own object. Often, but not always, and the failure of democratic institutions, where they have failed, has been due to lack of sufficient faith in democracy to create democracy. In Italy, Germany, Austria the faith has been only a small part of the total man. Its strength has been quickly exhausted. Man, as the Catholic Church understands him, has reasserted himself. With, or without the Church, hierarchies and privilege return.

Huxley criticizes the idea of equality and shows that men are not equal. Similarly, he criticizes Marxists and near-Marxists for assuming that if every one is given more money and more education, every one can be turned into the Alphas of a Brave New World. Of course, one recognizes, they cannot. But the Marxist equally, in a calm moment, detached from practical considerations, would recognize the same. I have frequently heard hard-working members of the Communist party say so. The point is that the Marxist hardly ever does have a calm and detached moment. His sense of ill in the existing world is so great that his ideal world necessarily over-compensates that ill. As a motive for action, to achieve a practical end, the revolutionary will set up an ideal whose complete achievement he would have to admit, if he ever visualized it to himself, was impossible. Thus, to destroy existing classes, you aim at a classless society, and so strong is your hatred of those existing classes that you really believe a classless society is possible. But seventeen years after the death of the Tsar, when the hatred-of-Tsarism motive no longer holds so strongly, you find that a new system of classes has established itself.

But because man's acts do not entirely conform with his faith, that does not mean that man should abandon the faith. Because democracy is imperfect, those who desire it should not yield to autocracy and despair, but persist in the faith and thus create its own object. Huxley says that revolutions have always disappointed the hopes of the revolutionaries. I do not think this is true, but even if it were, it would not be a reason for ceasing to revolt. I do not think it is true because I believe that the hopes of revolutionaries are actually much more modest than their public statements would suggest.

'The humanitarian democrats who affirm that men are equal, and who on the strength of their belief distribute votes to everybody, can claim no experimental justification for their beliefs and actions,' says Huxley. 'They are men who have a faith and who act on it, without attempting to discover whether the faith corresponds with objective reality.'

Huxley holds that this proceeding is wrong. Logically, he is obviously right. But he is, it seems to me,

realistically wrong because his view of the objective
reality is incomplete.   It is easy, by pointing to the
specialized functions of man, to show that men are
patently not equal.   It is easy to show that man is
not free, not independent, that reason is not equal
in all men.   It is quite easy to demonstrate all this
even without the help of Jung's *Psychological Types*.
But when man's inequality and bondage have been
admitted, the whole has not been said.   Man is not
always *ventre à terre*. In the life of every individual there
come moments when the sense of man's humanity,
of man's lonely and tragic estate, overrides all individual distinctions, moments almost of a mystical
nature when we feel that it is easy and necessary to
love our neighbour.   Tom, Dick and Harry may be
respectively a liar, a coxcomb and a well-meaning
fool, but there are times when we agree with tears that
' a man's a man, for a' that.'   And with some men
and women more abundantly gifted than others with
love and pity, these moments extend to the abiding
conviction of years.   Equally with nations there are
times when a sense of human unity, intensified by the
unity of nationality, floods over all individual differences.   What separates man from man suddenly
seems insignificant beside what joins man to man,
what is unlike beside what is like.   These emotions
are as real as the ' vertical and horizontal ' differences
in mankind.   They may not be the whole of man,
but they are a vastly important part.   Men may not
always love their neighbour, but they all think that
they ought to.   And what a man thinks he ought to

do is as much a part of him as what he actually does, and influences what he actually does. Democracy is based on what man thinks he ought to do. It does not correspond, if you like, with 'the objective reality,' if your view of that reality is a restricted one. But even if democracy does not correspond, even if it is, from a purely rational view, a lie, it is a lie profoundly valuable to mankind. By establishing the forms, habits and ceremonies of freedom and equality, democracy may actually create those states, even as the forms, habits, and ceremonies of the Roman Catholic Church have been known to create faith in the unbeliever.

It would be easy to quote from Huxley to show that he was in favour of Fascism, whereas his political 'prejudices' are in fact 'mildly Fabian,' and 'in favour of democracy, self-determination, and all the rest of it.'

For instance such a passage as the following:

'Plenty of people, as I shall show later, are interested in the local or vocational politics that affect their daily lives. And they are not only interested in them; they are well qualified to handle these small problems successfully. But few, on the contrary, are interested in national and international politics; and fewer still are qualified to cope with the major problems of statesmanship.'

This reads very much like the opening remarks of a defence of the Fascist ideal of the corporate state.

The objection may be made to such a theory as this
that men's private prejudices and interests will almost
certainly warp their judgement of local and vocational politics, whereas owing to their personal
remoteness from big national and international affairs
they are able to give unprejudiced judgments in
these matters, once they have clearly grasped the
issues involved. It is in this latter aspect of the
problem that the difficulty for democracy arises.
Big political issues are seldom presented to the public
with the impartiality, for instance, of a judge's sum-
ming-up in a criminal case.

Huxley does, no doubt, incline towards the Fascist
ideal in that, as he says, he prefers any efficient government to an inefficient one. But this decision is
theoretical. Shown an efficient Fascist government
in practice, as in Italy, he finds that he dislikes it
intensely, while his analysis of the psychological
foundations of Nazi Germany in *Beyond the Mexique
Bay* leave little doubt as to his opinion of *National-
sozialismus*. Very interesting too as a revelation of
unexpected irrationalism is a passage in *Jesting Pilate*,
dealing with the question of Swaraj.

'Moreover,' he says, 'even if, as an Indian, I
shared the Englishman's belief, even if it could
somehow be proved that Swaraj would bring, as
its immediate consequences, communal discord,
religious and political wars, the oppression of the
lower by the higher castes, inefficiency and corruption, in a word, general anarchy—even if this

could be proved, I think I should still go on trying to obtain Swaraj. There are certain things about which it is not possible, it is not right to take the reasonable, the utilitarian view.'

Huxley's conception of the ideal form of government, which he outlines in *Proper Studies*, is an intellectual aristocracy. A country should be ruled by the best of its citizens. At present, the administrative side of governments are in this. sense aristocratic. Admission to the civil service requires a high standard of education and intellectual ability. But in the legislature no such qualifications are necessary. All that is needed is wealth or the power of demagogic persuasion. 'Sometimes a few good men appear among the riff-raff of law-makers, sometimes the riff-raff is unadulterated. Fate chooses; we do not.' Huxley suggests, therefore, that to improve the quality of the legislature the same tests should be applied as are found necessary for the civil service. At the same time the vote should only be given to those who can pass a fairly stiff intelligence test.

These are intended as elementary reforms, based on established practice in many other spheres of activity, which would constitute a first step in the direction of government by those best fitted to govern. At the same time, it is appreciated that different excellences are required for the different tasks involved in the work of government. 'The man who can deal personally and directly with men is by no means necessarily the most intelligent; he may be able to lead,

but incapable of deciding which way to lead.' It
follows, therefore, that ' Leaders will be chosen, but
strictly confined to their job of leading—unless of
course they also happen to possess political insight.
The politically intelligent and well informed will make
the plans ; but unless they happen to have some talent
for personal command or blandishment they will never
come out into the open where they might risk making
fools of themselves among their fellows.'

In this connection the organization of an army is
instructive, although ' A state in all respects like an
army would be a horrible thing.'   In the army leader-
ship is separated from planning.   The aristocratic
state should have its chief of staff as well as its officers
among the ranks.

Together with the essay on *Political Democracy*
which reaches the conclusions above indicated, should
be read that on *Revolutions*, in *Do What You Will*.
Some remarks in this read a little curiously now, five
years after it was published.   For example : ' In
America, under modern capitalism, the whole Proletariat is prosperous and well organized.'   The essay
aims at showing that the facts of history have proved
Marx to be wrong in his theory of historical development.   That theory depended, says Huxley, on the
continued existence of the Proletariat.   But ' The
Proletariat as he knew it has ceased—or, if that is too
sweeping a statement, is ceasing—to exist in America,
and, to a less extent, industrialized Europe.'   The
present trend, says Huxley, is towards the gradual
absorption of the Proletariat into the bourgeoisie.

This movement will go on, because 'it pays the capitalist to have a prosperous Proletariat about him.' Thus the Proletariat may confidently expect to get from capitalism those material benefits which Socialism has hitherto alone offered to provide. 'So that, if the present tendency continues, it would seem that the danger of a strictly communistic revolution in the highly developed industrial countries, like America, will disappear.'

Do What You Will was published in 1929. The essay quoted was evidently written before the Great Slump. Throughout it adopts the viewpoint of Fordian economics, of spending for prosperity. In *Beyond the Mexique Bay* Huxley realizes that the apparent disappearance of the American Proletariat was only a disappearance behind a façade—the elaborately built-up façade of American 'prosperity.'

It may legitimately be objected to the belief in the gradual disappearance of the Proletariat that it does not take into account the possibility of the creation of a new Proletariat from the influx of country-born workers into the towns—a process which appears to be widespread, if not universal. Even in the U.S.S.R., where agriculture is under governmental control, special measures have had to be taken to limit the drift to the towns.

Revolutions is the longest discussion of Marxism in Huxley's work. His criticism of Marxian economics I have displayed. Certain articles in *The Sunday Referee* (July 1 and 22, 1934) contain interesting reflections on the problem of liberty in Marxist Russia.

The value of private property, he points out, is that it ensures some degree of freedom from governmental interference to those who possess property. In a country like France, where property is widely distributed, a comparatively large part of the population will enjoy a measure of freedom. But in a Communist society, though theoretically it offers the most just system of distribution of property, governmental interference need have no limits.

'It is for this reason,' says Huxley, 'that the great French Socialist Proudhon advocated the retention, under any scheme of Socialism, of a limited right to private property.

The principle, I believe, is sound ; only on the lines laid down by Proudhon can the world hope to enjoy the advantages of Liberalism at the same time as the advantages of Socialism.'

What is, by implication, a theoretical justification of certain methods of governing employed by the Soviets is contained in Huxley's review of the Federation of Progressive Societies and Individuals' *Manifesto* in *Plan*, July 1934. After referring to the 'Samurai' which H. G. Wells used to advocate, Huxley says :

'The fact that the advocates of a given policy or ethic are disinterested people trained up in habits of austere self-discipline, is in itself no guarantee of the intrinsic excellence of that policy or that ethic. But it does undoubtedly render the policy or ethic more generally acceptable. If people were

profoundly stirred by the preachings of the Fran-
ciscans, of Savonarola, of the early Jesuits, it was
to a great extent because they respected the preachers
as being better than themselves. . . . The creation
of a caste of Samurai is a piece of strictly practical
politics.'

It would seem that it is for this same reason that
the members of the Russian Communist Party are so
respected in their own country, and for this very
reason that the Russian people were so moved by
Lenin and other Bolshevik preachers. In all first-hand
accounts of the U.S.S.R. given by even moderately
sympathetic persons, it has been made clear that
the actual members of the Communist Party of the
U.S.S.R. are more hard-working, devoted, and con-
scientious than the majority of citizens. The numbers
of the Communist Party of the U.S.S.R. are severely
restricted. Its ranks are not open to all and every one.
There are periodic purges of inefficient members. A
great deal of unpaid and often thankless work is
expected of Party men. Their private lives have to
be morally impeccable. Drunkenness and promiscuity are much graver misdemeanours in the Party
ranks than out of them.

Similar in purpose and effect are those who are
' Shock Brigaders ' (volunteer workers), members of
the Young Communist League and so on. These
are the Samurai of Soviet Russia. It is undoubtedly
thanks largely to them that Communism has triumphed
there in the face of terrifying obstacles.

Huxley continues :

' There is even a great deal to be said for the creation of a caste of Brahmins above the Samurai. Their immediate, political, propagandist value would be less than that of the more active Samurai ; but ultimately, it seems to me, society can derive nothing but benefit from the existence of such a caste.'

This too the U.S.S.R. has put into practice. What but members of a Brahmin caste are the highly paid, even subsidized novelists and poets of the Soviet Union, scientists like Pavlov, film producers like Pudovkin and Eisenstein ? The Russian novelist Babel, for instance, has written nothing for years, but he continues to receive a salary. The Soviet appreciates the value of its Brahmins.

Much would be done to remove the imperfections of English Communism if our own Brahmins, men of the quality of Huxley and Aldington and E. M. Forster, would look more carefully into Communism and consider whether they cannot, after all, find it worthy of support. They would in all probability discover, as André Gide did, that they could support it.

Proper Studies contains, besides the political essays, one on education which seems to me wholly admirable. After criticizing existing systems, Huxley expounds with approval the Dalton system. I do not know what the majority opinion among schoolmasters is on the Dalton system, but my experience of the modified form of it used by some of the masters at

University College School was, that while admirable
for the boy already possessing independence and
initiative of mind, it was useless for the less self-
confident boy. Such a boy definitely did not like
being left to work in his own way. He felt lost,
bewildered, if he were given a month's work and told
that he could do it how and when he liked, so long as
it was done in the time. He much preferred to be
supported on a minutely apportioned time-table of
small tasks, rather than to be left to make his own
methods, his own discipline of working. The little
self-confidence he had disappeared altogether under
such a system. If the master saw his difficulty and was
able to interfere just sufficiently, while not disturb-
ing the principle of the method, doubtless such a boy
profited in the end.   Like all superior methods, the
Dalton plan demands superior persons to operate it.

The essay concludes with a brief speculation on the
education of the future.   ' A perfect education,' says
Huxley, ' is one which trains up every human being
to fit into the place he or she is to occupy in the social
hierarchy, but without, in the process, destroying his
or her individuality.'

The difficulty is, of course, that the social hierarchy
is always changing.   Thus, as Huxley himself points
out elsewhere, the caste of priests dwindles, and that
of doctors, psycho-analysts, and artists grows.   Peas-
ants give place to factory-workers, a surplus of which
may eventually give rise to a new grade of land-
workers.   And so on.

In his introduction to John Henry Burns's *A*

Vision of Education, Huxley speculates on what will happen when the resources of the earth, owing to man's wastefulness, will have seriously diminished. He suggests that then a termite-like organization of humanity will be necessary, because to preserve the species will be the over-riding purpose of mankind. Under such conditions 'individualism will mean hunger, and the pursuit of personal happiness and self-expression will lead to more misery than insect-like self-sacrifice to the Genius of the Species.'

Such a termite organization of society Huxley has described in *Brave New World*. The preservation of the species from destruction through war was the motive in that case.

But for the increasing 'termitism' of our own industrial West there seems to be no motive, except the profit one. Therefore, 'present-day education and present-day social arrangements put a premium on the citizen and immolate the man. On all those human tendencies which do not make for good citizenship, morality and social tradition pronounce a sentence of banishment.'

The problem for education in the future will be to reconcile the specialized functions of man with his human and animal nature. For the few there is, as a temporary measure, the way outlined in *Do What You Will*. For the many there is Communism.

*   *   .*

Beyond the Mexique Bay, Huxley's account of a journey to Central America, contains, among a multitude of speculations, a long and valuable essay on the psychological causes of war. Some of the ideas in this essay Huxley put before a larger audience in his broadcast address in the late autumn of 1934 on ' Sadist Satisfactions in War.' The address was also published in *The Listener* for November 14, 1934.

It seems to me that in these reflections on the causes of war Huxley has contributed to the general stock of ideas on the subject something of value and fundamental necessity. Pacifists, Socialists and Communists alike, in their discussion of war, seldom turn from the consideration of other people's wickedness to a consideration of their own. They leave out of account the whole question of Original Sin.

Other ages were wiser in this matter than our own. The Roman Catholic Church showed by its practice that it recognized that man is naturally cruel, naturally sadistic, that he naturally delights in inflicting pain, on himself as well as on others. The blood sacrifice is inherent in the blood of man. The centuries of evolution have not yet bred out of him this ancient primitive desire for pain, cruelty and death. Like love and religion it is an approach to the infinite. Caught up in the ecstasy of cruelty, man feels, as in the ecstasy of the flesh or of God, that he is more than man. And like love and drunkenness and religion, this ecstasy too has its mornings after. More terrifying mornings, an infinitely deeper gloom than the sadness which follows the bed, the sourness the bottle, and the weariness the prayer. It is this which has perhaps kept men from tasting this ecstasy too often.

That and a trembling foreboding, a terror of its destructive efficacy. Man cannot stand for long the infinity which cruelty gives. Its ultimate climax is the orgasm of death. Hence the dread and the fascination which it inspires.

It is to this deep-rooted Original Sin of man that Huxley draws attention in his writings on war. He comes to it somewhat obliquely. A natural tendency to oppose the fashionable leads him to criticize, insecurely, it seems to me, the economic interpretation of war. In place of that interpretation he sets up a psychological one. I do not think his criticism of the economic doctrine goes very deep, but, at the same time, I feel that what he says on the psychological theme is of the greatest importance.

Briefly, then, what Huxley says is this.

Wars are the product of passion. The capitalist rulers are as much the slaves of passion as the ruled. These war-producing passions are hatred, vanity and the gregarious instinct. Nationalist doctrines are a theology for maintaining these passions when they would, left to themselves, have normally subsided. The ordinary rhythm of human life is 'Routine punctuated by orgies.' Nationalism justifies the emotional orgies of hating, boasting and union with the mob, which are a psychological necessity for the majority of mankind.

'The fundamental problem of international politics is psychological. The economic problems are secondary and, but for the psychological problems, would not exist. . . . To attempt to cure symptoms, such as tariff-wars and armaments, without at the same time attacking the psychological causes of these symptoms, is a proceeding fore-doomed to failure. What is the use of a disarma-ment or a World Economic Conference so long as the people of each nation are deliberately en-couraged by their leaders to indulge in orgies of group-solidarity based on, and combined with, self-congratulation and contemptuous hatred for foreigners? Our need is rather for a World Psychological Conference, at which propaganda experts should decide upon the emotional cultures to be permitted and encouraged in each state and the appropriate mythologies and philosophies to accompany these emotional cultures.'

Whether the economic problems are secondary or not, there is no doubt that the psychological problems are of the greatest importance. The very existence of these problems is seldom realized.

The task of the World Psychological Conference which Huxley proposes would be to find some means of providing the vast masses of urbanized, emotion-craving people with the excitement they demand while at the same time avoiding the destructive after-effects of war.

It might be questioned whether people really do demand excitement as much as Huxley says they do. A conclusive reply seems to be given by the suicide statistics. During the Franco-Prussian War, and still more in the World War, only about seventy people committed suicide for every hundred who did so in peace time. 'The suicide statistics seem to show,' says Huxley in his broadcast address, ' that, for non-combatants at any rate, life in war-time is about forty-five per cent. more worth living than in times of peace.'

There is further the observable fact that the number of people who feel emotionally stirred by the League of Nations is very small, whereas the number of those who hate the foreigner, the Jew, the capitalist, the Bolshevik, and at the same time are terrifically proud of being British or 'Nordic,' or inhabitants of 'God's own country,' is enormous. 'Hatred and vanity pay a higher dividend in psychological satisfaction than do impersonal benevolence and reasonableness.'

Granted that people must have excitement, how is it to be provided ?

In the first place, it may be observed that all governments, though they encourage the passions of vanity and hatred, deplore and discourage those of sexual lust. What is necessary is that the collective passions should be made as discreditable as the private ones. (It is possible that it would even be worth while deliberately encouraging these private passions, if it would obviate the collective ones.)

But since mere moral propaganda will never suffice, men's natural rivalry must be diverted into harmless channels. Such are, for example, rivalry in industry, much exploited in the U.S.S.R. Rivalry in sport sublimates a certain amount of bellicose passion. We need, too, more shows, pageantry, circuses to enliven the dullness of day-to-day existence, such as Hitler and Mussolini have employed with such effect, but without, naturally, the nationalist moral of their circuses.   The difficulty would be to make the shows significant as well as picturesque.   In this country the wedding of a royal personage provides a harmless and very satisfying circus.

A shared hatred is a powerful unifying force.   Thus hatred of Hitlerite Germany may unite the rest of Europe.   Or hatred of Japan might unite Europe against Asia.   More likely, it seems to me, is a hatred of Communism uniting capitalist Europe against the U.S.S.R.   The only thing which would unite the world would be fear of attack from Mars.

But without a shared hatred to prevent even parts of the world from breaking into mutually destructive fragments, something could be done to remove the psychological causes of war.

The Mayas of Central America, the Chinese, the inhabitants of India, lived for centuries without having recourse to militant nationalism.   They were able to do this, says Huxley, referring to Central America, because the natural rhythm of life was satisfying. Routine was secure and the organized emotional stimulations, chiefly of religion, were thoroughly satisfying.

In the modern world, routine is boring and the excitements of poor quality.

' Nationalism is harmful, but satisfying; and even war itself, if we may judge from what happens to the suicide rate, may be for many individuals a source of substantial pleasure. The problem is to find a substitute for these two institutions—in other words, to sublimate the impulses which at present find satisfaction in nationalism and war. Sport and other competitive activities can doubtless be made to fill at least part of the gap. Much too could be done by making civilized life less monotonous. It is boredom that makes the emotional orgies of group feeling, vanity and hatred seem so delightful. Abolish boredom and you abolish one of the main psychological reasons for nationalism, and so, indirectly, for war.'

Chapter 6

CRITICISM

Critics, it seems to me, content themselves too often with the mere application of epithets.

T. H. Huxley as a Man of Letters.

HUXLEY'S criticism, though small in quantity, is particularly interesting because it gives us an indication as to the angle from which his creative work should be regarded. From his *Vulgarity in Literature*, *Music at Night* and *Along the Road* we may understand why he writes as he does. Informative too, in a different way, is his *T. H. Huxley as a Man of Letters*, a lecture delivered at the Imperial College of Science. A certain amount of criticism is to be found also in the novels, especially in *Point Counter Point*, some examination of which has already been made.

Huxley is, by nature, a natural historian who finds his material, not among the coleoptera, but among civilized mankind. He is a 'collector of human specimens.' The only things he finds worth collecting are 'psychological varieties.' Like other contemporary writers he finds it impossible to write pure tragedy ; he is too much aware of ' the great oceans of irrelevant things, events and thoughts ' surrounding any element in life he may chose to contemplate. His aim in writing is therefore naturalistic. Not naturalistic in the sense that Tchehov or Defoe are naturalistic, but in the sense that ' Literature is also philosophy, is also science. In terms of beauty it enunciates truths. . . . Naturalistic works contain the more detailed beauty-truths of particular observation.' Huxley's criticism explains the methods and effects of this kind of literature, ancient as well as modern, and in so doing it explains one of the most important characteristics of his own work.

The central essay in his criticism is that in *Music at Night*, entitled *Tragedy and the Whole Truth*.

In this essay Huxley makes an illuminating distinction between literature which seeks to tell the Whole Truth and literature which tells only the Partial Truth. To explain what is meant by this distinction he takes as an example of the Whole Truth in literature an episode from the *Odyssey*—the conclusion of the story of Scylla's attack on the ship. Homer, he points out, does not bring down his curtain on the survivors weeping for the death of their friends. He goes beyond that. He shows the sailors eating and drinking as well as weeping. He tells how they prepared their supper ' expertly,' and that only when they had satisfied their hunger and thirst, did they weep. And after that ? After weeping, says Homer, they fell asleep. In short, Homer insists that even in the extreme of grief men retain their human needs. Homer is a writer who tells the Whole Truth. In this he differs from the writer of tragedy. If he had been writing a tragedy he would have told only part of the truth, would have excluded from the scene everything but the tears. Tragedy, says Huxley, is a distillation from experience. It is a concentrated essence. It owes its quick and powerful effect to the fact that it is, as it were, chemically pure. And at the same time, no doubt, the sense of unreality which we sometimes feel about tragedy is due to this fact, that it is too pure.

The works of writers like Homer who tell the Whole Truth are never tragical. Another such writer is Fielding.

'*Tom Jones*,' says Huxley, 'is one of the very few Odyssean books written in Europe between the time of Aeschylus and the present age ; Odyssean, because never tragical ; never—even when painful and disastrous, even when pathetic and beautiful things are happening. For they do happen ; Fielding, like Homer, admits all the facts, shirks nothing. Indeed, it is precisely because these authors shirk nothing that their books are not tragical. For among the things they don't shirk are the irrelevancies which, in actual life, always temper the situations and characters that writers of tragedy insist on keeping chemically pure.'

Huxley's own novels abound in instances of this admission of irrelevancies. A good example in *Point Counter Point* is on page 335—the scene in which Elinor Quarles returns home from India and is eagerly hoping to meet her little son on the doorstep. Instead they drive up to a deserted porch. The front door of the house is open. It is a house where ' three and a half centuries of life had gone to sleep.' Ancient, mellow, serenely beautiful—the house

is all these. ' Like the Sleeping Beauty,' Elinor said.
But even as she says it, comes disenchantment, the
everyday irrelevancy : ' Somewhere upstairs a door
opened, through the sanitary noise of rushing water
came the sound of Phil's piercing young voice. . . .'

That homecoming might have been made lyrically,
chemically pure. Huxley prefers to tell the Whole
Truth. There is a distinct gain in the sense of realism,
of closeness to the nature of things.

To many these irrelevancies seem unpleasant, disagreeable in a novel. It is admitted that they exist in
life; but art, for the majority, is only acceptable in so
far as it is superior to life. The popular successes of
the films and of fiction are seldom of the Wholly
Truthful kind. It would never do for the heroine at
the thrilling passionate moment to turn away in disgust
because the hero has bad breath. What is known as
' B.O.' may exist in American life ; it is impossible
in American films. Popular taste is all for either
comedy or tragedy, because both are simple, hit
straight home, demand only one narrowly limited
response. Popular taste does not like comedy and
tragedy mixed. This is no doubt the reason why
so very few important contemporary writers are
widely popular, for all such writers do mix their moods.
Huxley mentions five—Proust, D. H. Lawrence,
André Gide, Kafka, Hemingway—all different, and
yet all alike in that they have none of them written a
pure tragedy. And all alike, one might add, in that
none of them is truly popular. They are not, because
they are all interested in the Whole Truth.

What then, we may ask, are the virtues of this kind of writing, as opposed to the virtues of literature of the Partial Truth, the literature of Tragedy?

'Tragedy,' says Huxley, 'refines and corrects and gives a style to our emotional life, and does so swiftly, with power. . . . From the reading or the hearing of a tragedy we rise with the feeling that

> Our friends are exultations, agonies,
> And love, and man's unconquerable mind;

with the heroic conviction that we too would be unconquerable if subjected to the agonies, that in the midst of the agonies we too should continue to love, might even learn to exult.'

This is, incidentally, the best short elucidation of the pleasure we take in tragedy that I have ever come across. It makes sense of the Aristotelian theory of catharsis, with which it agrees, and it disposes of the sterile controversy as to whether catharsis should be translated purgation or purification, by appreciating that either idea includes the other. Primitive tribes in many parts of the world, as may be learned from *The Golden Bough*, have many elaborate rituals of purification through purgation in its most physical sense. We know that the Greek drama arose out of an almost world-wide ritual, and the language which served for the one must necessarily have cast its shadow on the language which later served for the other. It seems merely reasonable to suppose that the ideas of purgation and purification were closely associated in the word catharsis. Aristotle, no doubt, meant either or both. ' What is the difference ? ' he would have asked, if pressed for a more precise definition. In his actual teaching he may well have dwelt further on the point. But that we shall never know. The *Poetics* is, after all, only a lecturer's notes.

Huxley's explanation of the pleasure in tragedy is so good because, like Aristotle's, it is simply a description of what happens when one sees or reads a tragic story. We can easily check the account by referring it to our own experience. And, to speak for myself, Huxley's account corresponds exactly with experience.

Tragedy is felt to be valuable, then, because of the mood of heroic exultation it produces. The mood, incidentally, soon passes. The day after we have, with tears in our eyes, heard Horatio say :

' Now cracks a noble heart ! Good-night, sweet prince,
And flights of angels sing thee to thy rest ! '

we are as unheroic as ever. The tears of painful joy have gone, and we wonder how we ever shed them.

The virtues of Wholly Truthful art are different. It does not work so rapidly and powerfully as Tragedy, but, says Huxley, its effects are more lasting. The mood which results from it is one of resignation, of acceptance of the world, rather than of fierce exultation. To achieve this effect, ' Wholly-Truthful art overflows the limits of tragedy and shows us, if only by hints and implications, what happened before the tragic story began, what will happen after it is over, what is happening simultaneously elsewhere. Tragedy is an arbitrarily isolated eddy on the surface of the vast river that flows on majestically, irresistibly, around, beneath and on either side of it. Wholly-Truthful art contrives to imply the existence of the entire river as well as of the eddy.'

At the present time writers are interested in this kind of literature and not in tragedy. There is a slump in chemically pure art, which only exists on an inferior level in the work of popular writers.

Another contrast to Wholly-Truthful art is provided by the aesthetic convention known as classicism. This convention may be briefly defined as the geometricalization of passion. The convention is to be seen in its most extreme form in French classical tragedy. The plays of Racine are a reduction of particulars to universality. In them man no longer has a body. He is simply a discarnate passion.

In Huxley's view the classical convention, with its insistence on unity, its rigorous lopping-off of all side-lines and side-issues, its rejection in short of all irrelevancies, is, despite its formal difficulties, an escape from the greatest difficulty which confronts a writer. That difficulty is ' to render adequately, in terms of literature, that infinitely complex and mysterious thing, actual reality.'

The French classicists would have claimed, no doubt, that they represented a higher reality than that of appearance. After all, they had Plato, Aristotle and the Roman Catholic Church to teach them about higher realities. But that, Huxley objects, as we have already seen, is a mental abstraction which may or may not coincide with ' reality ' as perceived by

'God.' All we can actually know is our psychological life in all its complicated diversity: 'the
consciousness of events which we have immediately,
through our senses and intuitions and feelings, is
incomparably subtler than any idea we can sub-
sequently form of that immediate consciousness.'

A certain amount of simplification is, evidently,
necessary, otherwise there could be no art at all.
The naturalistic writer, however, endeavours to simplify as little as possible. ' His ambition is to render,
in literary terms, the quality of immediate experience
—in other words, to express the finally inexpressible.
To come anywhere near achieving this impossibility
is much more difficult, it seems to me, than, by elim-
inating and simplifying, to achieve the perfectly
realizable classical ideal.'

He adds further on the suggestive remark : ' Incidentally this world of relationships ' (*i.e.* between man
and the world about him), 'this borderland between
"subjective" and "objective," is one which literature
is peculiarly, perhaps uniquely, well fitted to explore.'

Huxley himself has done this, and superlatively,
but clearly what he calls ' naturalism ' is not the whole
of Huxley. He has, as he says, 'a taste for the lively,
the mixed and the incomplete in art.' What he mixes
with the naturalistic is the baroque, the fantastic, in
a sense the romantic. He is, in this respect, a mixture
not unlike Flaubert, but with a larger dose of science
than Flaubert had.

It has always seemed to me that the novels which
Huxley, with one part of himself, desires to write

are admirably described in that fanciful passage
of *Crome Yellow* about the imaginary Tales of
Knockespotch :

' Oh, those Tales—those Tales ! How shall I
describe them ? Fabulous characters shoot across
his pages like gaily dressed performers on the
trapeze. There are extraordinary adventures and
still more extraordinary speculations. Intelli-
gences and emotions, relieved of all the imbecile
preoccupations of civilized life, move in intricate and
subtle dances, crossing and recrossing, advancing
retreating, impinging. An immense erudition and
an immense fancy go hand in hand. All the ideas
of the present and the past, on every possible subject, bob up among the Tales, smile gravely or
grimace a caricature of themselves, then disappear
to make place for something new. The verbal
surface of his writing is rich and fantastically
diversified. The wit is incessant.'

Of Huxley's novels, *Those Barren Leaves* probably comes nearest to the Knockespotch ideal, while
of the pleasure of writing in the baroque style he
gives an amusing account in *Vulgarity in Literature*.
On the same subject he also has some wise remarks in
Along the Road.

' The baroque style and the kindred romantic
style,' he says, ' are the two styles best fitted in the
nature of things for the expression of comedy.
Aristophanes, Rabelais, Nashe, Balzac, Dickens,
Rowlandson, Goya, Doré, Daumier and the

nameless makers of grotesques all over the world and at every period—all practitioners of pure comedy, whether in literature or art—have employed an extravagant, baroque, romantic style.'

It is questionable whether all the names given were practitioners of pure comedy all the time. Balzac, Dickens and Goya were certainly not. But it is nevertheless true that these artists are most successful when their style is employed for comic purposes. And one at least—Dickens—is only endurable when he is being comic. He and Balzac well illustrate the truth of Huxley's subsequent remark : 'Except in the hands of prodigious men of genius (such as Marlowe and Shakespeare, Michelangelo and Rembrandt) this style when used for serious purposes, is ludicrous.'

The clearly-drawn distinction which Huxley makes between the styles of Brunelleschi and Alberti, those of Piero della Francesca and Tura, and his essay on Wren in *On the Margin* reveal that he has a penetrative eye for the intrinsic qualities of the plastic arts, while *Point Counter Point* and the very beautiful title essay of *Music at Night* are eloquent of his appreciation of music. Huxley's criticism seldom deals with contemporary artists, and when it does it reveals occasional surprising ignorances. Thus in the essay on *Subject Matter of Poetry*, in the 1923 *On the Margin*, he says : 'The twentieth century still awaits . . . its up-to-date Laforgue '—and is apparently unaware of T. S. Eliot, although *Prufrock* is of 1917 and *Poems* of 1920.

Huxley is deeply interested in the technics of
writing, and yet his criticism contains little on this
subject, probably because what he has to say is to be
found in his actual practice, in the novels, poems and
short stories. He excels above all in relating literature and art to the society which produced them, in
considering them as social phenomena. This may be
seen especially in *Beyond the Mexique Bay*, with its
account of Mayan sculpture and other Central
American arts, and in numerous essays in *On the
Margin*. Consider, for instance, those on *Modern
Folk Poetry* and *Democratic Art*, which may be
regarded as social investigations of which the final
fruit is to be found in the hypnopaedic rhymes and
the Solidarity Service of *Brave New World*, or that on
Advertisement, which is the seed of a long and fantastically humorous passage in *Antic Hay*.

Huxley's longest essay on literary technics is the
lecture on his grandfather as a writer. This is indeed,
though little known, a most interesting piece of work.
The following paragraph contains advice from the
following of which English criticism would be greatly
benefited :

' Critics, it seems to me, content themselves too
often with the mere application of epithets. . . . But
this is not enough. Critics should take pains to show
why such and such a piece of writing provokes us
to call it by such and such a name. The observable
facts of literature are words arranged in certain
patterns. The words have a meaning independent

of the pattern in which they are arranged; but it is the pattern which gives to the meaning its peculiar quality and intensity; that can make a statement seem somehow truer or somehow less true than the truth. Moreover, a word-pattern of one kind will cause us to say of its inventor: " This man is (for example) sincere " ; of another kind: " This man is affected and false." It is the business of the literary artist to make word-patterns in such a way that his readers shall be compelled to draw certain inferences from them. It is the business of the critic to show how our judgments are affected by variations in word-patterns.'

This is advice which should, but almost certainly will not be taken to heart by most critics of the newspapers and periodicals. If more attention were paid to the manner and less to the matter of contemporary writing, there would be less windy inflation of literature, and the bad money would not drive out the good quite so successfully as it does at present. Of one recently much-boosted novel—Mr. Anthony Thorne's *Delay in the Sun*—only one critic in the newspaper press had the wit to point out that a book which contained the (almost unbelievable) phrase, ' The urgent manhood of his limbs,' could not possibly be other than fundamentally insignificant. But as Huxley pertinently says :

' To a sensitive critic the judgments passed on books by quite intelligent and highly educated people often seem bewildering in their irrelevance and apparent perversity. He hears them speaking of utterly dissimilar works, as though there were nothing to choose between them. One happens to be refined and another vulgar ; one genuine and another manifestly a fraud and a forgery. But such trifling differences seem to pass quite unnoticed.'

Every one who knows anything about art or literature must have observed this most definitely bewildering phenomenon. It is made all the more baffling because to the person of taste nothing seems easier than to distinguish between the genuine and the sham, between the work of art and the other productions which, whatever their qualities, are simply ' non-art.' That is to say, they are not simply less good varieties of art, but something altogether different in kind.

Chapter 7

TRAVEL BOOKS

... it is practically impossible to travel without being sometimes bored.—*Along the Road.*

THE snobbery motive for travel has always existed. After reading Huxley's lively dissection of this motive in *Along the Road* it is comforting to find in the seventeenth-century writer, James Howell, this observation on travellers :

'They strive to degenerate as much as they can from Englishmen, and all their talk is still foreign, or at least will bring it to be so, though it be by head and shoulders, magnifying other nations, and derogating their own. Nor can one hardly exchange three words with them at an ordinary (or elsewhere) but presently they are th'other side of the sea, commending either the wines of France, the fruits of Italy, or the oil and salads of Spain.'

The snob of the ' They-order-these-things-better-in-France' type has a long ancestry. Clearly, too, he was always as much a bore as he is now. James Howell must have suffered badly from the man who button-holed him at his ordinary. Ideally, one should be charitable with such bores. For travel has done some good to the commender of the wines of France. It has kept him from completely insular self-satis-

218

faction. Doubtless he has simply acquired another kind of complacency, but if he goes on travelling long enough, he may at last emerge into a decent appreciation of his own as well as of other countries.

'Why not stay at home?' Huxley asks, without expecting any drearily serious answer. 'With me,' he cheerfully replies, 'travelling is frankly a vice. The temptation to indulge in it is one which I find it almost as hard to resist as the temptation to read promiscuously, omnivorously and without purpose.' Actually, is there any need for an answer? One might as well expect an answer to the question, why eat apricots? Travelling has a pleasant taste. That, really, is all there is to it.

To Bacon it was obvious that you travelled to acquire knowledge. For the artist, whether in paint or language, travel is valuable, I suppose, because it adds so richly to the mind's store of images, provides new symbols for one's emotions. Six months in Morocco gave Delacroix the imaginative ferment of a lifetime. He lived in Africa for the rest of his life. Into his brain it was packed; the brazen sunlight, the date-palms, the white houses with courtyards where a fountain endlessly falls, the shadowed lanes roofed with vines, the slow, veiled women, and the long, tawny sea of the desert, till at last he could have Africa about him whenever he would. In the end Delacroix was able to paint tigers where none exist—among the African sands. But those tigers of Delacroix's imagination are stronger and fiercer and more magnificent than the tigers of reality. They would prowl away victorious from any combat with a mere tiger of India or an actual lion of Africa. Out of Delacroix's travels in Morocco those tigers were born, in one of the dark alleyways opening on the desert—one of many memories in his crowded store of images.

Those tigers in Africa are a symbol of Delacroix's romanticism. Similarly, travel was valuable to Lawrence, because it gave him the terms to express something that was actually inside himself. He would, no doubt, have expressed it even if he had lived in Nottingham all his life, but the expression would have been restricted and repetitive. Travel enabled Lawrence to say the same thing many times without becoming a bore.

In a rather different way travel enables Huxley to speak his mind on a great variety of topics without ever becoming a bore, either to himself or the reader. Many things in one's daily experience are worth a brief note, but are too slight for a whole essay. At the same time, they would be a digression in a novel. They cannot be digested into a poem, a play or a short-story. Only in the travel-book can these intractable fragments of experience be comfortably dealt with. This is the aim and achievement of Huxley's two travel books *Jesting Pilate* and *Beyond the Mexique Bay*.

These books are related, in kind, to such ostensible books of travel as Voltaire's *Lettres Philosophiques* or Johnson's *Journey to the Western Islands of Scotland*. They have not much in common with the books of H. M. Tomlinson, or D. H. Lawrence's writings about foreign and distant parts.

Lawrence's *Plumed Serpent, Mornings in Mexico* and other works made us all more than usually aware of the Central American Indian. What was before only a vague shadow became a palpitatingly alive figure. Since Lawrence's death that Indian has perhaps retreated somewhat into his native obscurity again. His real position for us may possibly be found by comparing Huxley's reaction with that of Lawrence.

Thus, Lawrence, describing a Mexican Indian, writes :

' And yet, it was only his eyes that mattered. They were black and of extraordinary piercing strength, without a qualm of misgiving in their demonish, dauntless power. He looked into the eyes of the white woman with a long, piercing look, seeking she knew not what. She summoned all her strength to meet his eyes and keep up her guard. But it was no good. He was not looking at her as one human being looks at another. He never even perceived her resistance or her challenge, but looked past them both, into she knew not what.'

Huxley, confronted by those same Indian eyes, says :

' Lifting his chin a little, he blew, for perhaps the eight-hundredth time that morning, the first notes of " Who'll buy, who'll buy." Above the barrel of his whistle his eyes stared fixedly into space, black like boot-buttons and no less perfectly inexpressive. I found myself suddenly rather disquietingly reminded of a photograph I had once seen of a giant tortoise eating a snake. The serpent hung, like so much living spaghetti, from those toothless and scissor-like jaws, and the tortoise's eyes were gazing with a bright, unwinking fixity into the *Ewigkeit*. Two round black nothings focussed upon nothing. . . . It was the same here at the church door in Ciudad Vieja. Nothing gazed at nothing. The drum beat; the thin squeaking of the melody dropped to its conclusion; then, for the eight hundred and first time, began again. And still, above the penny whistle, those black buttons beamed with the same impenetrably meaningless brightness.'

Lawrence is an introvert, Huxley an extravert. It is obvious that Lawrence is himself seeking in the Indian ' he knows not what.' The Indian is the alphabet in which he tries to spell out something he has obscurely glimpsed within himself. But Huxley, on the other hand, knows all about what is going on within him; there are no particular mysteries there. He has no temptation to use the Indian as a symbol. He sees him quite flatly and sharply as he is—something that to outward appearance is almost entirely animal. Lawrence's savages are tremulously alive, but it is by no means certain that they live with the actual life of savages. It is much more likely that the breath in them is that of Lawrence's imagination. Huxley gives only the outside of the savage, but there is no disputing that. It is a fact of experience, verifi-

able by observation in a way that Lawrence's ' demonish, dauntless power ' is not verifiable. But to
get correctly even only the outside of something is an
achievement not to be despised.

The description of landscapes does not play any
large part in Huxley's travel books. And when he
does describe, he is apt to give only a rough and
summary account of what is before him. He excels
most in the rendering of effects of light, as for instance this, from *Jesting Pilate* :

> ' There are days in our northern winter, still
> days, windless, sunless and, from morning to even-
> ing twilight, uniformly illumined under a white-
> grey sky, days when the whole bare country seems
> to glow, or to be just on the point of glowing, with
> an intensity of suppressed colour. It is as though
> a brown and earthy light were striving to break
> from under the clods of every ploughland ; the
> green of the winter grass is a sulking emerald ; and
> the leafless trees and hedges, which seem at first
> glance merely black, are seen by the more discern-
> ing eye as the all but opaque lanterns through which
> a strange, strong, quivering radiance of deepest
> plum colour is almost vainly shining.'

This is a spectacle seen with the painter's eye. It
explains admirably the reason for what to many seems
a fantastic heightening of colour in the landscapes of,
for instance, Cézanne, or Van Gogh. There are days
even in London when, the longer one gazes at the
trees in Ken Wood, the more it seems impossible ever

to find blues and purples in paint vivid enough to parallel reality.

And when you have travelled round the world, what have you gained ?

Huxley found that only after much journeying was he deeply and intimately convinced ' that it takes all sorts to make a world, and that the established spiritual values are fundamentally correct and should be maintained.'

Travel ' inculcates tolerance, but it also shows what are the limits of possible toleration. . . . All men, whatever their beliefs, their habits, their way of life, have a sense of values. And the values are everywhere and in all kinds of society broadly the same. Goodness, beauty, wisdom and knowledge, with the human possessors of these qualities, the human creators of things and thoughts endowed with them, have always and everywhere been honoured.'

Chapter 8

POETRY

. . . it is only by poets that the life of an epoch can be synthesized.—*Texts and Pretexts.*

HUXLEY'S poetry is, so far as I know, unique among contemporary poetry in that it is scientific. That is to say, his poetry is the poetry of a man who is as much moved by a scientific idea as by a human emotion. In this it has something in common with some of the noblest that has been written—with that of Lucretius, Dante and Donne.

There have been numerous attempts in the past at writing poetry about scientific matters. English versifiers of the eighteenth century were adepts at producing splendours like—in a poem about hygiene —'And some do use to take the gelid cistern,' while even Alfred de Vigny could describe the locomotive as 'Le taureau de fer qui fume, souffle et beugle' or as a 'dragon mugissant.' The trouble with these combinations of science and poetry was that the result, as a rule, partook of neither ingredient. This problem of scientific poetry, which is one of great interest, and one which Huxley is particularly well qualified to discuss, is dealt with in *On the Margin* (Subject Matter of Poetry), and still more brilliantly in *Music at Night* ('And Wanton Optics Roll the Melting Eye ').

' Poetry,' says Huxley, ' can be made out of science, but only when the contemplation of scientific facts has modified the pattern, not only of the poet's intellectual beliefs, but of his spiritual existence as a whole—his " inscape," as Father Hopkins calls it.'

It will not, I think, be disputed that science has profoundly modified Huxley's ' inscape.' And his poetry, as much as his novels, reflects this modification. One of the best of his scientific poems is this, from *The Cicadas* :

SHEEP

' Seeing a country churchyard, when the grey
Monuments walked, I with a second glance,
Doubting, postponed the apparent judgment day
To watch instead the random slow advance
Across the down of a hundred nibbling sheep.
And yet these tombs, half fancied and half seen
In the dim world between waking and sleep,
These headstones browsing on their plot of green,
Were sheep indeed and emblems of all life.
For man to dust, dust turns to grass, and grass
Grows wool and feeds on grass.   The butcher's knife
Works magic, and the ephemeral sheep forms pass
Through swift tombs and through silent tombs, until
Once more God's acre feeds across the hill.'

The epigrammatic concision of that last line, the packed meaning of the conceit, makes the whole sonnet. I like too the phrase 'postponed the apparent judgment day.'

Another treatment of the same idea is *Meditation* :

' What now caresses you, a year ago
Bent to the wind that sends a travelling wave

Almost of silver through the silky corn
Westward of Calgary; or two weeks since
Bleated in Gloster market, lowed at Thame,
And slowly bled to give my lips desire;

.   .   .   .   .   .

My future body, which in Tuscan fields
Yet grows, yet grunts among the acorns, yet
Is salt and iron, water and touchless air,
Is only numbers variously moved,
Is nothing, yet will love your nothingness.'

The theme of these poems is one which has greatly fascinated Huxley. It is treated also in *Point Counter Point*.

Towards the beginning of the novel (p. 39) Lord Edward Tantamount is described idly turning over the pages of the *Quarterly Review*. A quotation from Claude Bernard strikes his eye: 'The life of the animal is only a fragment of the total life of the universe.' His attention is excited. Suicide, then, he reflects, is impossible. ' What was one day a sheep's hind leg and leaves of spinach was the next part of the hand that wrote, the brain that conceived the slow movement of the Jupiter Symphony. And another day had come when thirty-six years of pleasures, pains, hungers, loves, thoughts, music, together with infinite unrealized potentialities of melody and harmony had manured an unknown corner of a Viennese cemetery, to be transformed into grass and dandelions, which in their turn had been transformed into sheep, whose hind legs had in their turn been transformed into other musicians, whose bodies in their turn . . .'

The two poems quoted give a more concise, more penetrating expression to the same train of thought.

In his introduction to *Texts and Pretexts* Huxley remarks : ' I like things to be said with precision and as concisely as possible.' In saying that he is describing the best qualities of his own poetry. He excels in the compact and memorable phrase. His poetry would have been much appreciated by readers of the Metaphysical poets of the seventeenth century. He is, in temper, very like Donne, but a Donne in whom science replaces alchemy and uncomfortable scepticism uncomfortable faith. If Donne had written novels, they would, one feels, have been very similar to Huxley's. Donne's *Ignatius His Conclave or His Inthronation in a Late Election in Hell : Wherein Many Things are Mingled by way of Satyr* is a very fair essay in the Peacock manner, or that of *Crome Yellow.*

Important as an influence in the creation of this style of Huxley's was the work of Laforgue. Laforgue's mingling of ' remote discovery with near sentiment' may be paralleled in Huxley. Compare :

' Celle qui doit me mettre au courant de la Femme !
    Nous lui dirons d'abord, de mon air le moins froid :
    " La somme des angles d'un triangle, chère âme,
        Est égale à deux droits." '

with Huxley's poem *Male and Female Created He Them,* which contrasts Corydon's thoughts with

Diaphenia's ecstatic delight as he makes love to her.
'Luncheon to-day cost three and two,' he thinks as
he strokes her thorax.   She says :

> ' Corydon !
> I faint, faint, faint at your dear touch.
> Say, is it possible . . . to love too much ? '

Similar in its juxtaposition of learned fact and
human emotion is the *Second Philosopher's Song*,
which is based on the assertion of Pliny that a drowned
man drifts face upwards, but a drowned woman face
downwards, or the *Ninth Philosopher's Song* which
regrets the birth of the author out of ' a million
million spermatozoa ' instead of a new Shakespeare,
Newton or Donne.

Huxley makes considerable use of words which,
like ' spermatozoa ' at first sight appear intractable to
poetry.   A number of such more or less technical
terms may be noted.   But they have to be looked for.
They in no way stand out as irrelevant to the texture
of the verse ; there is no question of scientific em-
broideries on commonplace ' poetic ' themes.   The
scientific words come naturally to Huxley's pen—
words like *mucus, kidney, thorax, cancer, sliding
weights, recession, aquarium, neap, delta*, yield vigorous
and expressive metaphor or simile.   Two of his most
striking images are violently physiological :

> ' Mind, issued from the monkey's womb,
> Is still umbilical to earth,'

> ' Unearthly lightnings leap across the sky
> Like sudden sperm.'

Besides Laforgue, other important influences for Huxley were Rimbaud, Corbière, and Baudelaire. The influence of the latter poet seems particularly strong in the sonnets in *The Cicadas* volume. These sonnets—there are fourteen of them, mostly fairly late in their date of production—seem to me Baudelairean in their weighty, stone-like richness of form, as well as in their mood, which is often a mood of despair of a kind that Baudelaire would have felt congenial. Perhaps the finest of these sonnets is :

MEDITERRANEAN

' This tideless sapphire uniformly brims
Its jewelled circle of Tyrrhenian shore.
No vapours tarnish, not a cloud bedims,
And time descending only more and more
Makes rich, makes deep the unretiring gem.
And yet for me who look on it, how wide
The world of mud to which my thoughts condemn
This loathing vision of a sunken tide !
The ebb is mine.   Life to its lowest neap
Withdrawn reveals that black and hideous shoal
Where I lie stranded.   Oh deliver me
From this defiling death !   Moon of the soul
Call back the tide that ran so strong and deep,
Call back the shining jewel of the sea.'

In this and in several other poems in *The Cicadas* Huxley describes a state of spiritual lassitude not unlike those ' plaines de l'Ennui, profondes et désertes ' which were such a fruitful inspiration to Baudelaire.

Arabia Infelix, for instance, portrays the calcined land where all the emotions are dried up and despair of rain :

' Faithless the cloud and fugitive ;
　An empty heaven nor burns, nor wets ;
　At peace, the barren land regrets
　Those agonies that made it live.'

In one of the sonnets he writes :

' The thunder calls and every spasm of fire
　Beckons, a signal, to that old desire
　In calm for tempest and at ease for pain.'

He fears the ' silting of the soul ' and longs for
' the lost continent of tears and mirth,' and for those
waters of life, ' those humbler streams, whose source
is earth, is earth and not our dreams.'

He writes of himself as in a sepulchre, waiting for
life :

' They do not come ; have rolled away the stone,
　But lie unrisen, lie unvisited.
　Merciful God, bid them to come again !
　Sometimes in winter
　Sea-birds follow the plough
　And the bare field is all alive with wings,
　With their white wings and unafraid alightings,
　Sometimes in winter.   And will they come again ? '

He thinks that ' All seems achieved, dried up the
source of things.' He is resolved :

' No more to hope, but only to remember :—
　Let there be silence round the slumbering will,
　And when time beckons, turn away your face.'

And yet, despite the weariness, the hopelessness,
the final note of the volume is one of courage, albeit
desperate courage :

' The choice is always ours.   Then, let me choose
　The longest art, the hard Promethean way

> Cherishingly to tend and feed and fan
> That inward fire, whose small precarious flame,
> Kindled or quenched, creates
> The noble or ignoble men we are,
> The worlds we live in and the very fates,
> Our bright or muddy star.'

To which may be added his version of the teaching of Lawrence :

> ' Clueless we go ; but I have heard thy voice
> Divine Unreason ! harping in the leaves,
> And grieve no more ; for wisdom never grieves,
> And thou hast taught me wisdom ; I rejoice.'

As regards the influence of Corbière, it appears to be principally a rhythmical one. Corbière's emphatic quatrains seem to have affected Huxley's rhythms now and then. At least, one seems to hear the heavy lilt of :

> ' Bénite est l'infertile plage
> Où, comme la mer, tout est nud.
> Sainte est la chapelle sauvage
> De Sainte-Anne-de-la-Palud.'

in Huxley's :

> ' For oh, the lily and the mud !
> Fair is still fair and foulness, ill.
> With her, on her, what you will.
> This fire must be put out with blood.'

or :

> ' Hot wind from this Arabian land
> Chases the clouds, withholds the rain.
> No footsteps print the restless sand
> Wherein who sows, he sows in vain.'

In the *Leda* volume, published in 1920, the influences, besides Laforgue, whom we have already dealt with, are Rimbaud and Marlowe. There is not much to be said on either topic. Rimbaud inspired the style of the prose poems in this book, in one of which Huxley sets forth his ideal of beauty.

' It is,' he says, ' not a far-fetched, dear-bought gem ; no pomander to be smelt only when the crowd becomes too stinkingly insistent ; it is not a birth of rare oboes or violins, not visible only from ten to six by state permission at a nominal charge, not a thing richly apart, but an ethic, a way of belief and of practice, of faith and works, mediaeval in its implications with the very threads of life. I desire no Paphian cloister of pink monks. Rather a rosy Brotherhood of Common Life, eating, drinking ; marrying and giving in marriage ; taking and taken in adultery ; reading, thinking, and when thinking fails, feeling immeasurably more subtly, sometimes perhaps creating. . . .

Ventre à terre, head in air—your centaurs are your only poets. Their hoofs strike sparks from flints and they see both very near and immensely far.'

The influence of Marlowe is to be observed in the title poem which describes how Jove, feeling exceptionally celibate in Heaven, where

' Libido like a nemesis
Scourged him with itching memories of bliss '

changes himself into a Swan, and with the help of

Aphrodite, who becomes an eagle, succeeds in arousing pity in the breast of Leda, which pity soon turns into desire, with satisfactory results for Jove.

The poem is a very brilliant piece of work, mingling rich and suave description with delightful touches of humour and realism, but to me, at least, it is too much a poetical exercise to be really interesting. There is more sting, more vivid life in the satirical pieces of the same volume.

In the introduction to *Texts and Pretexts* Huxley regrets that he has not the abilities of Dante, so that he might write a new Divine Comedy of contemporary civilization. Though he doubts whether even Dante could have written his work under present conditions. And yet it ought to be done. We need a synthetic view of the modern world, and ' it is only by poets that the life of an epoch can be synthesized.'

Huxley would not claim that his own poetry had achieved this synthesis. Not his poetry—but the claim might with much justice be made for the novels. *Brave New World* and *Point Counter Point* will, if you let your memory feel for them, come back into the mind as two fiery and passionate poems summing up contemporary life in Western Europe and America. One is a fierce lyrical song and the other a vast symphony which stirs reverberations in the mind long after it was heard and seemingly forgotten.

Chapter 9

STYLE

I have always been interested in the subtleties of literary form.—*On the Margin.*

Some psychologists affirm that the smile comes before the pleasurable emotion. In the same way there is, it seems to me, a sense in which a writer's style comes before his thought. Such and such a style will permit a man to think only in a certain way. Some thoughts he will be able to have, and others he will not, on account of his style. ' Style,' says Ernest Dimnet, ' is the gestures of an author's expression,' thereby implying that one may express without gestures, and alternatively, make gestures without expressing.

I should, perhaps, have chosen to begin, rather than to finish this book, with an account of Huxley's style. For without pressing a notion too far, I hold that Huxley's thought has been to some extent conditioned by the style which he early formed for himself by the writing of light and consistently entertaining essays for *The Athenæum.* Those lively ' middles ' of *On the Margin* are undoubtedly partially responsible as well for the philosophy of balanced excess as for the general character of his writing. For the successful essayist must be multifarious. He must hold to nothing with fanaticism. If he does, he ceases to hold the reader. He may be single-minded in nothing but

scepticism. And, Huxley ruefully confesses, ' the
necessity under which he labours of always being
readable tempts him at all costs to be original and
unusual.'

Huxley took his job as a periodical essayist with
great conscientiousness. Those essays of *On the
Margin* are, to me, at least, the most readable and
re-readable short pieces produced by any contemporary author.

Out of this necessity and this achievement of
readableness arose Huxley's style, and with it the
kind of thoughts which it would allow Huxley to
think.

Huxley's prose is a kind of very brilliant and
cultivated conversation. Its peculiar texture, with its
balancing of generalization and particular example, of
statement and re-statement, has the rhythm of conversation among a small but choice group of cultured,
intelligent and uninhibited men and women, all
familiar with each other, all able to catch every allusion
to a common past, and each an expert on some branch
of human culture, always ready to contribute his or her
drop of fine essence to the final rich fragrance. The
characteristics of Huxley's style, observable in a
sentence, extend on parallel lines through paragraph,
page, a whole essay, a whole book.

The movement of the prose is a parallelism, like the
movement of Hebrew poetry. Successive metaphors
present the same fact from a variety of view-points.
Concrete example parallels abstract generalization. A

simple statement made in this way glistens with refracted light.

Let us take an example from *Point Counter Point* (page 119):

> 'Like all professional talkers Molly was very economical with her wit and wisdom. (There are not enough *bons mots* in existence to provide any industrious conversationalist with a new stock for every social occasion. Though extensive, Molly's repertory was, like that of other more celebrated talkers, limited. A good housewife, she knew how to hash up the conversational remains of last night's dinner to furnish out this morning's lunch. Monday's funeral baked meats did service for Tuesday's wedding.)
>
> To Denis Burlap she was at this moment serving up the talk that had already been listened to with such appreciation by Lady Benger's lunch party, by the week-enders at Gobley . . .' etc.

Now, for the purposes of the transition from a general statement about Molly to a particular instance, the section I have put in parentheses is, from the point of view of an economical stylist, superfluous. Prosper Mérimée, for instance, would have regarded it as mere elaboration, eloquence. But notice what richness and life is added to our conception of Molly as a conversationalist by those bracketed sentences.

First there is a generalization about the cardinal difficulty of the conversationalist's profession. Then a plain statement about Molly, linking her with this profession. This point is emphasized by a metaphor from domestic science which, because of its incongruity with the character of Molly d'Exergillod, catches the mind the more sharply. Lastly, this metaphor is finally thrust home by the allusion to Hamlet, which is singularly effective because of its unexpectedness. Those four sentences which follow the plain statement of Molly's economy make it impossible for us ever to forget this characteristic of hers. The whole passage is an admirable example of that kind of baroque writing which is, as Huxley says, so suitable for comedy.

In the passage just quoted the general and the particular run side by side, in parallel separate sentences. And this is, as a rule, the normal structure of Huxley's prose. It is a development of the structure so much employed by Sir Thomas Browne, a structure which differs from Huxley's in that his parallelism is within the sentence, thus :

' The various Cosmography of that part hath already varied the names of contrived constellations : *Nimrod* is lost in *Orion*, and *Osyris* in the Dogge-starre.'

Generally, in Browne, one gets a parallelism, not of general and particular, but of related generalizations.

Huxley, in the lecture on his grandfather referred to earlier, comments on T. H. Huxley's use of this ' caesura sentence ' employed by Sir Thomas Browne, and gives as an example :

'Ignorance is visited as sharply as wilful dis-
obedience—incapacity meets with the same punish-
ment as crime.'

This is of the same form as :

'To burn the bones of the King of Edom for
lime, seems no irrationall ferity ; but to drink of
the ashes of dead relations, a passionate pro-
digality.'

In Aldous Huxley the structure becomes this :

'These single-minded revivalists of Christianity
did more to preserve the stability of English institutions than all the Tory politicians. The greatest
conservatives of the age were not the Wellesleys,
but the Wesleys.'

Or this :

'But though black is not with us a sacred colour,
black images of exceeding holiness are none the less
fairly common in Europe. The reason, I suspect,
is that such statues have a somewhat sinister appearance. (The Holy Face of Lucca is very nearly
black, and with its glittering jewelled eyes, is one
of the strangest and most terrifying sculptures ever
made.) In Otto's terminology, black idols are
intrinsically more " numinous " than white. Num-
inosity is in inverse ratio to luminosity.'

Or this :

'If all men were alike, all the world would worship the same God. Aphrodite, however, bears

little resemblance to Calvin's Jehovah, Siva is
singularly unlike the Something not ourselves that
makes for the righteousness of cultured modernists.'

It will be observable how the rhythm of Aldous
Huxley's sentences has not the emphasis, the sonorous
weight of Sir Thomas Browne's, or even of T. H.
Huxley's. It is really less a sentence rhythm than a
paragraph rhythm. Browne's paragraphs are an
accumulation of ' caesura sentences,' each of which
may be detached from the whole passage without
great loss. But to detach Huxley's sentences in this
way is difficult. To give the full effect of the last of
the three examples just given, I should really have
quoted almost the whole page. Huxley's rhythm
is, in contrast to that of Sir Thomas Browne, light
and broken.

' Un article,' says Rémy de Gourmont, ' peut
être un poème, dès qu'on lui a assigné le rythme sur
lequel il déroulera sa brève pavane. Le rythme
trouvé, tout est trouvé, car l'idée s'incorpore à son
mouvement, et le peloton de fil ou de soie se forme
sans que la conscience d'un travail soit quasi
intervenue.'

There is little doubt that Gourmont, who wrote so
much, composed in that manner. And very often—
perhaps almost always in his essays—Huxley appears
to compose in the same way. His thought is guided
by the words. He has a habit of seizing upon some
word or phrase, usually grotesque and odd or striking

in some way and using it as a melodic phrase or brief
rhythmic figure again and again throughout an essay.
The phrase is introduced, it disappears for a page or
two, reappears in a new context, and so on, giving
musical form to the whole piece. A good example is
that delightful parody of a sermon in *Crome Yellow*,
where the fantastic word 'knops' becomes more
absurdly comic with each repetition. Another example is the essay *Subject Matter of Poetry* in *On the
Margin*. Here, the melodic phrase is the word
'Bohunk':

> '. . . contemporary poets can now write, in the
> words of Mr. Sandburg, of . . . "wops and
> bohunks." . . . Where Homer wrote of horses
> and the tamers of horses, our contemporaries write
> of trains, automobiles, and the various species of
> wops and bohunks who control the horse-power.'

Then, two pages further on :

> 'It is not enough to have written about loco-
> motives and telephones, "wops and bohunks"
> and all the rest of it. . . . The critics who would
> have us believe that there is something essentially
> unpoetical about a bohunk (whatever a Bohunk
> may be) . . .'

On the next page :

> 'And the critics who think it very new and
> splendid to bring bohunks into poetry are equally
> old-fashioned in their ideas.'

By the time we have reached this sixth repetition of the grotesque word, we are convinced for ever and ever that all poets and critics who have anything whatever to do with bohunks—impossible word!—are eternally damned. Bohunk, again and again repeated, convicts of folly as no reasoned argument could. Its authority is incontestable.

For an example of the use of a whole sentence in this way, we may turn to *Vulgarity in Literature*. Here it is a quotation from Villiers de l'Isle-Adam :

' *Vivre ? Nos valets le feront pour nous.*'

The remark begins a paragraph on page 9, which continues :

' For, oh, the vulgarity of it ! The vulgarity of this having to walk and talk ; to open and close the eyes . . .' and so on for fourteen lines, to conclude :
' it simply wasn't done. *Vivre ? Nos valets le feront pour nous.*'

On the next page, a clever pun reminds us of the same idea : ' For a corpse is, by definition, a person absolutely devoid of *savoir vivre.*'

Two pages later we come across it again :
' *Vivre ? Nos valets le feront pour nous.* But the physicists and psychologists have revealed the universe as a place, in spite of everything, so fantastically queer, that to hand it over to be enjoyed by footmen would be a piece of gratuitous humanitarianism. Servants must not be spoiled. . . .'

The four repetitions of the original phrase, and several variations on the phrase, occur in some five or six pages. They give to the passage the quality

of a strongly rhythmical piece of music, or, to take
an image from another art, they are like

> ' the grave
> And stoical recession, row on row
> Of equal columns.'

This kind of composition, with its constant re-
introduction of the same text in a variety of sur-
roundings, resembles the method of composition
traditionally employed for sermons by Donne and
many other preachers. It may briefly, if paradoxi-
cally, be defined as a kind of expansive concision ; or
alternatively, as a steady digression towards the same
point.

The opening of Huxley's introduction to Lawrence's
Letters is exactly like the opening of a sermon :

' " I always say, my motto is ' Art for my sake.' "
The words are from a letter written by Lawrence
before the war. . . .'

The next paragraph begins, similarly :

' " Art for my sake." But even though for my
sake, still art. . . .'

The vast superiority of Huxley's sermons over
those of the contemporary Church may be seen in the
fact that the ideas which he is able to extract from his
text far exceed in width of scope and in number the
ideas of the professional preacher. He has only to
note an idea, and it proliferates rapidly into a vast
foliage, like the Biblical seed of mustard sprouting
into a lodging for the fowls of the air. Sometimes
this method which, at its best, yields a crop of
subtle and ingenious shadings on the original outline,

becomes instead the mere hammering in of a point
sufficiently clear at the first statement. When that
happens (as in some of the essays of *Proper Studies*)
the sermon becomes somewhat tediously obvious.
Born in the ages of Faith, Huxley would have been one
of the most famous of divines, famous for his learning
and his eloquence. His gift for absorbing and being
able to use information of the most diverse kinds, his
capacity for always being able to produce an example
in support of any statement of theory or principle,
his firm, tough and flexible style could all have been
used with the greatest effect in the service of the
Church. The twentieth-century Huxley's mustard
trees which spring from one scientific, sociological
or psychological observation would have sprung as
readily from a line of Holy Writ.

Ultimately the distinction of a man's mind is to be
known, not from the matter, but from the manner
of his writing.

'. . . the amount of knowledge, the singularity of
facts, even the novelty of discoveries,' said Buffon,
'are no sure guarantees of immortality. . . . These
things are beyond the power of man, style is man
himself.'

'Man himself.' The phrase sums up Huxley's style
to perfection. His style is an epitome of all that is
most distinguished in human life, of all that is best in
European culture since the Renaissance. It has no
contact with the ages of Faith, little with the interests
of those ages. You may search his writings in vain

for any important allusion either to the Old or the New Testaments—but it shares most splendidly the qualities of the Renaissance and of the archetypal land of the Renaissance—Italy.   The richness of the Italian landscape, the ripe sensuous intellectuality of Italian painting, sculpture and architecture have permeated his prose style.   Even when he is treating of some abstract subject—aesthetics, psychology or sociology—his writing has a warm sheen, a deep luxurious quality of superb velvet.   Like Gourmont, Huxley takes in handling ideas ' a physical pleasure akin to caressing a shoulder or a piece of stuff.'   In essays dealing apparently only with the Orders of Pascal or the prospects of a Shavian Utopia, the pages glow with a mysterious radiance, whose source is imperceptible, like wine, like silk, rose-petals or translucent marble.

Chapter 10

BIBLIOGRAPHY

Personally, I am the friend of any edition which is reasonably well printed and bound, reasonably correct in the text and reasonably clean.—*On the Margin.*

WORKS OF ALDOUS HUXLEY IN CHRONO-LOGICAL ORDER OF PUBLICATION [1]

1916

The Burning Wheel. (Poems.) pp. 51. 8vo. This is No. 7 of: 'Adventures All.' (A series of young poets unknown to fame.) B. H. Blackwell, Oxford. 1916-1920.

1917

Jonah. Christmas 1917. pp. 14. 8vo. Holywell Press, Oxford. About fifty copies were printed.

1918

The Defeat of Youth, and other poems. pp. 48. 8vo. This is No. 3 of: 'The Initiates: A series of poetry by proved hands.' B. H. Blackwell, Oxford.

The English Poets, Vol. V. Edited by Thomas Humphrey Ward. The selection of poems by John Davidson, Ernest Dowson and Richard Middleton and the critical introductions on these writers were by Aldous Huxley. Macmillan and Co., London.

[1] I am greatly indebted to Mr. Basil Menhinick for his help in compiling this bibliography.

1920

Limbo. (Six stories and a play.) pp. 292. Chatto and Windus. 8vo. First published January 1920. Fifth printing January 1924. Contains: Farcical History of Richard Greenow, Happily Ever After, Eupompus Gave Splendour to Art by Numbers, Happy Families (a play), Cynthia, The Bookshop, The Death of Lully.

Leda, and other poems. pp. 80. Chatto and Windus. 8vo. First published April 29, 1920. Reprinted May 1920, August 1922, October 1926.

The New Keepsake for the Year (Le Nouveau Keepsake pour l'Année) 1921, edited by X. M. Boulestin. Contains: Imaginary Conversation—Kenelm and Venetia Digby, by Aldous Huxley. London, Paris, 1920. 8vo.

1921

A Virgin Heart, by Rémy de Gourmont. Translated by Aldous Huxley. pp. 230. 8vo. N. L. Brown, New York.

Crome Yellow. (A novel.) pp. 325. Chatto and Windus. 8vo. First published November 1921. Fifth printing April 1927.

1922

Mortal Coils. (Four stories and a play.) pp. 229. Chatto and Windus. 8vo. Some of the stories had previously appeared in *The Cornhill, The English Review, Coterie*. First published April 1922. Third printing February 1925. Contains: The Gioconda Smile, Permutations Among the Nightingales (a play), The Tillotson Banquet, Green Tunnels, Nuns at Luncheon.

Job le Pauvre by Jean de Bosschère. Traductions des poèmes en anglais, et quatorze gravures noires. Translation of: Dès que l'homme ne sera plus père, by Aldous Huxley. pp. 124. 8vo. John Lane, London.

1923

On the Margin. Notes and Essays. pp. v, 229. Chatto and Windus. 8vo. First published May 1923. Third printing February 1926. A note says: 'Most of these essays appeared in *The Athenæum* under the title MARGINALIA and over the signature AUTOLYCUS. The others were first printed in *The Weekly Westminster Gazette*, *The London Mercury* and *Vanity Fair* (New York).'

Antic Hay. (A novel.) pp. 328. Chatto and Windus. 8vo. First published November 1923. Fifth printing February 1927. The page following the title-page bears the quotation:

My men like satyrs grazing on the lawns
Shall with their goat-feet dance the antic hay.
                                                MARLOWE.

1924

Little Mexican, and other stories. pp. 340. Chatto and Windus. 8vo. First published May 1924. Third printing February 1927. Contains: Uncle Spencer, Little Mexican, Hubert and Minnie, Fard, The Portrait, Young Archimedes.

The Discovery. A Comedy in Five Acts written by Mrs. Frances Sheridan. Adapted for the modern stage by Aldous Huxley. pp. 121. 8vo. Chatto and Windus. Most of the last act consists of new material by Aldous Huxley.

1925

Those Barren Leaves. (A novel.) pp. 379. Chatto and Windus. 8vo. First published January 1925. Fourth printing January 1927.

Along the Road. Notes and Essays of a Tourist. pp. viii, 259. Chatto and Windus. 8vo. First published September 1925. Third impression May 1927.

Selected Poems. pp. 63. Basil Blackwell, Oxford. 8vo.

The Opportunities of a Night, by Jolyot de Crébillon. Translated by Eric Sutton from ' La Nuit et le Moment.' With an introduction by Aldous Huxley. pp. xxv, 187. 8vo. Chapman and Hall. This is No. 2 of the series ' Eighteenth Century French Romances.'

1926

Two or Three Graces, and other stories. pp. 271. Chatto and Windus. First published May 1926. Second impression June 1926. Contains: Two or Three Graces, Half-holiday, The Monocle, Fairy Godmother.

Jesting Pilate. The Diary of a Journey. (With plates.) pp. 291. Chatto and Windus. 8vo. First published October 1926. Third printing May 1928. The title-page bears the quotation:

> *What is Truth? said Jesting Pilate, and would not stay for an answer.* FRANCIS BACON.

Essays New and Old. pp. viii, 257. Chatto and Windus. 8vo. Twenty-eight essays, nine of which are published in book form for the first time. The remainder are from: *On the Margin*, and *Along the Road*. Edition limited to 650 numbered and signed copies.

The Autobiography and Memoirs of Benjamin Robert
Haydon, 1786-1846. Edited by Tom Taylor. A new
edition with an introduction by Aldous Huxley. 2 vols.
pp. xxxi, ix, 875. Pl. xii. Peter Davies.

A Virgin Heart, by Rémy de Gourmont. Translated by
Aldous Huxley. pp. 238. 8vo. G. Allen and Unwin.

Chatto and Windus Almanack, 1927. pp. 202. Roy. 8vo.
Contains: Jacques Callot, by Aldous Huxley. October
1926.

1927

Proper Studies. (Essays.) pp. xix, 299. Chatto and
Windus. 8vo. First published November 1927. First
issued in The Phoenix Library 1929. The title-page bears
the quotation:

> *The proper study of Mankind is Man.*—POPE.

1928

Point Counter Point. (A novel.) pp. 601. Chatto and
Windus. 8vo. The page following the title-page bears
the quotation:

> *Oh wearisome condition of humanity,*
> *Born under one law, to another bound,*
> *Vainly begot and yet forbidden vanity,*
> *Created sick, commanded to be sound.*
> *What meaneth nature by these diverse laws,*
> *Passion and reason, self-division's cause?*
>   FULKE GREVILLE.

The first edition contains a misprint on page 116, line 22,
where ' time ' is obviously in error for ' name.' This is
corrected in the cheap edition. Page 598, line 3 of the
first edition has the grammatical error, possibly a misprint, of: ' had passed from achieved perfection into
perfection yet *more deeper.* . . .'

Printing of To-day, by Oliver Simon and Julius Roden-
berg. An illustrated survey of post-war typography in
Europe and the United States. With a general introduction by Aldous Huxley. pp. xix, 83. 4to. Peter Davies ;
Harper and Bros., New York.

1929

Do What You Will. (Essays.) pp. 310. Chatto and
Windus. 8vo. First published in October 1929. Second
impression 1929. The title-page bears the quotation :

> *Do what you will, this world's a fiction*
> *And is made up of contradiction.*
>   WILLIAM BLAKE.

Holy Face, and other essays. pp. 64. With drawings
by Albert Rutherston. The Fleuron Press. 8vo.
Limited to 300 copies.

Arabia Infelix, and other poems. pp. 35. Fountain
Press, New York. Chatto and Windus, London. 8vo.
Limited to 692 copies.

A Vision of Education : Being an imaginary verbatim
report of the first interplanetary conference. By John
Henry Burns. With a preface by Aldous Huxley. pp. 112.
Williams and Norgate. 8vo.

1930

Brief Candles. (Short stories.) pp. 320. Fountain
Press, New York. 8vo. Limited to 800 copies.

Brief Candles. (Stories.) pp. 323. Chatto and Windus.
8vo. First published May 1930. Second impression
1930. Contains : Chawdron, The Rest Cure, The
Claxtons, After the Fireworks.

Vulgarity in Literature. Digressions from a Theme.
pp. 59. Chatto and Windus. 8vo. The first item in
The Dolphin Books series.

This Way to Paradise. A play in three acts by Campbell
Dixon from the novel *Point Counter Point*. pp. 101.
With a preface by Aldous Huxley. Chatto and Windus.
8vo.

1931

Music at Night, and other essays. pp. 146. Fountain
Press, New York. 8vo. Chatto and Windus, London.
8vo. pp. 269. First issued in The Phoenix Library,
1932.

The World of Light. (A comedy in three acts.) pp. 104.
8vo. Chatto and Windus.

The Cicadas, and other poems. pp. 63. 8vo. Chatto
and Windus.

1932

Brave New World. (A novel.) pp. 306. 8vo. Chatto
and Windus. Sixth impression 1933. The page following
the title-page bears the quotation :

> Les utopies apparaissent comme bien plus réalisables
> qu'on ne le croyait autrefois. Et nous nous trouvons
> actuellement devant une question bien autrement
> angoissante : Comment éviter leur réalisation défini-
> tive ? . . . Les utopies sont réalisables. La vie
> marche vers les utopies. Et peut-être un siècle
> nouveau commence-t-il, un siècle où les intellectuels
> et la classe cultivée rêveront aux moyens d'éviter les
> utopies et de retourner à une société non utopique,
> moins ' parfaite ' et plus libre.
>
> NICOLAS BERDIAEFF.

Texts and Pretexts. An Anthology with commentaries. pp. viii, 311. 8vo. Chatto and Windus.

Rotunda. A selection from the works of Aldous Huxley. Selected by Aldous Huxley. pp. vi, 1081. Chatto and Windus.

The Letters of D. H. Lawrence. Edited with an introduction by Aldous Huxley. Heinemann. 8vo.

T. H. Huxley as a Man of Letters. pp. 28. 8vo. Macmillan and Co. This is the Huxley Memorial Lecture, 1932, Imperial College of Science and Technology.

1934

Beyond the Mexique Bay. pp. 319. With 30 plates and map end-papers. 8vo. Chatto and Windus.

Pitch Lake. A story from Trinidad. By Alfred H. Mendes. With an introduction by Aldous Huxley. Duckworth.

INDEX